EMPATH & PSYCHIC ABILITIES:

AWAKEN YOUR INTUITION, TELEPATHY, & CLAIRVOYANCE + STOP ABSORBING NEGATIVE ENERGY & THRIVE AS A HIGHLY SENSITIVE PERSON (HSP) IN THE MODERN WORLD

ABIGAIL HARGREAVES

© **Copyright 2022 - All rights reserved.**

The content contained within this book may not be reproduced, duplicated or transmitted without direct written permission from the author or the publisher.

Under no circumstances will any blame or legal responsibility be held against the publisher, or author, for any damages, reparation, or monetary loss due to the information contained within this book; either directly or indirectly.

Legal Notice:

This book is copyright protected. This book is only for personal use. You cannot amend, distribute, sell, use, quote or paraphrase any part, or the content within this book, without the consent of the author or publisher.

Disclaimer Notice:

Please note the information contained within this document is for educational and entertainment purposes only. All effort has been executed to present accurate, up to date, and reliable, complete information. No warranties of any kind are declared or implied. Readers acknowledge that the author is not engaging in the rendering of legal, financial, medical or professional advice.

CONTENTS

Introduction	5

PART ONE
EMPATHS AND EMPATHY

1. What Is an Empath?	13
2. How to Become an Empath?	19
3. Empaths and Psychic Abilities	24
4. Empaths and Healing	26

PART TWO
PSYCHIC ABILITIES

5. Basics	47
6. Telepathy	52
7. Clairvoyance	60
8. Parapsychology & Other Research	64

PART THREE
INTUITION

9. What Is Intuition?	73
10. How to Awaken Your Intuition	77
11. Empaths and Intuition	101

PART FOUR
HIGHLY SENSITIVE PERSONS (HSPS)

12. What Is an HSP?	115
13. Strengths of HSPs	126
14. Challenges for HSPs	135

PART FIVE
HOW TO STOP ABSORBING
NEGATIVE ENERGY AND THRIVE IN
TODAY'S WORLD—GUIDED
MEDITATION

15. Guided Meditation Basics — 147
16. Techniques — 157
17. Scientific Backing of Meditation — 173
18. Guided Meditation and the Psyche — 182

PART SIX
HOW TO STOP ABSORBING
NEGATIVE ENERGY AND THRIVE IN
TODAY'S WORLD—GROUNDING

19. What Is Grounding — 207
20. Benefits of Grounding — 210
21. Grounding Techniques — 213

PART SEVEN
WORLD—CRYSTALS

22. Crystal Basics — 219
23. Crystals and Healing — 223

PART EIGHT
AFFIRMATIONS

24. What Are Affirmations? — 239
25. Benefits of Positive Affirmations — 243
26. Types of Affirmations — 245
27. A Few Hours of Affirmations — 251

PART NINE
SELF CARE FOR MYSTICS

28. What Is Self-Care? — 269
29. Types of Self-Care and How You Can
Practice Them — 271

INTRODUCTION

If you're viewing this, it guarantees you've spent your money wisely and you are going to get your investment back. This book is for anyone interested in learning more about how humans are more than a collection of molecular processes. Humans, according to this book, are spiritual beings that have special energies and latent powers that can make them hypersensitive to concepts outside of their typical range. If you're interested in clairvoyance, empaths, highly sensitive people, or psychic powers, you've come to the right place. This book will guide you on a quest to discover, understand, and even practice mystical mysteries. It will show you how these abilities may be effective instruments for personal well-being, especially in difficult circumstances such as those that we are facing with the COVID-19 pandemic.

Let's dive into what Psychic Abilities and Clairvoyance really are. When you imagine psychic powers, you might picture crystal balls and elderly women shrouded in shawls who allege to have been endowed with extraordinary abilities as a result of some ancestral hex. As entertaining as it may sound, it is not really what it means to possess psychic abilities. Psychic powers can manifest themselves in a variety of ways and infiltrate the minds of a wide range of people. Psychics are those who, unlike everyone else, profess to having extrasensory perception, which they utilize to predict other people's futures using various mediums. Clairvoyance is the term given to possession and use of psychic abilities.

Clairvoyance is a type of visual intuition in which the person who possesses this gift has metaphysical sight. In this context, "clair" refers to as clear and "voyant" refers to being able to see. This clairvoyant skill helps you access your soul's wisdom as well as the collective knowledge of every single spirit present in the cosmos, even those who have appeared in the past who have yet to emerge. You can receive intuitive knowledge via pictures, visions, colors, dreams, and even symbols should you possess the ability.

Clairvoyance has its right-side buddy, called Empath. An empath is an individual who is acutely sensitive to the feelings of people around them, to the extent that they can experience those feelings themselves. Empaths have a unique perspective on the world; they are highly conscious of others, their emotional needs, and what might hurt them. However, empaths aren't just about feelings. They can also sense another's intentions or what their moral scope may be. In simpler terms, empaths catch onto a lot of what people around them are going through.

The term "empath" comes from the word empathy, which refers to the skill to comprehend and experience another's emotions. As you would expect, an empath is somebody who transcends most people's experiences when it comes to empathy. They're highly tuned in, so much so, that in case of a lack of emotional boundaries, they can absorb other people's energy.

Although several people think that most everyone holds some level of psychic ability, this ability can manifest in a variety of ways. For certain folk, psychic aptitude presents itself as the ability to empathize with others. Empathy as a psychic experience ought not to be mistaken with empathy as a basic human emotion. Without having psychic empathy, most people can still experience empathy for others. The key distinction between the two is that a psychic empath is sensitive to nonvisual, nonverbal signs that another person is experiencing, such as pain, terror, or delight. It may be a question of sensing energy fields, or it could merely be a matter of "knowing" that the person is feeling a specific way regardless of the lack of evident signs.

Psychic empaths have honed their ability to perceive minute changes in other individuals' energy waves in numerous circumstances. Many empaths are good listeners, and they naturally gravitate toward jobs that allow them to use this skill to help others. These can include social work, therapy, energy work, and theology.

Another type of ability that we need to look at is that of highly sensitive persons (HSPs). An HSP is a word coined to explain a group of individuals whose brains analyze everything in great detail. This includes feelings, thoughts, and sensory input. As a result, they are more physically and emotionally sensitive than others. High sensitivity is seen as a natural and healthy character trait which, in essence, is just like any other personality trait.

HSPs are frequently labeled as "too sensitive." Being an HSP, in actuality, isn't a negative thing. It has obstacles, just like every other personality attribute, but it also has a lot of advantages. HSPs, for instance, excel at creativity, empathy, and the capacity to notice details that others overlook or draw connections that others miss.

Possessing any of the said spiritual abilities will enhance one's life in a number of ways. For example, being clairvoyant can help one make better decisions and avoid things/people/places that may harm them. Clairvoyance, empathy, or being an HSP often renders you more creative than the average person. This means that you will flourish in careers that involve creativity: painting, writing, singing, dancing, and so on. Having these abilities gives you the opportunity to be helpful. Physics can give others great advice, empaths can share the burden of heavy emotions with others, HSPs can absorb some of the negative energy from others. Their susceptibility to emotions and the spiritual world can help heal others.

This is just a tiny slice of what you're in for. If you wish to expand your mind, learn more about spirituality, and be able to tell whether you possess any psychic abilities, keep reading on.

PART ONE
EMPATHS AND EMPATHY

CHAPTER 1
WHAT IS AN EMPATH?

EMPATHY IS the root of the term "empath." Empathy refers to the ability to sympathize with others and understand their experiences from their point of view, as in the popular phrase "Put yourself in their shoes." You may sympathize with somebody without actually going through what they are dealing with. If a buddy loses a family member, for example, you would be able to comprehend their anguish even if you haven't gone through it yourself.

Empaths take empathy to a whole other level. They are persons who can not only understand but also experience other people's emotions as if they were their own. Regardless of whether they have experienced the death of a close relative, their friend's grief over the loss of a family member would become their own. Empathy isn't simply limited to sadness; they'd be able to perceive any emotion in individuals around them, which could in fact make them feel uncomfortable. Empaths can also detect whether or not another person is thinking about them. It all rests on a person's level of sensitivity. Empaths are very sensitive to emotions, allowing them to sense what is going on around them.

When it comes to romance or intimacy, empaths are often uneasy because they find it incredibly stressful. For an empath, romantic relationships have a great risk of becoming overpowering, particularly when they become very close. The reason for this is that empaths may sense their partner's pain in situations that may cause them tension. For example, an empath may desire alone time, but in the course of communicating that desire to their partner, they may get agitated due to their ability to sense their partner's pain. Closeness or intimacy might even cause sensory overload in empaths. The issue of sensory overload occurs when your five senses flood you with more information than your brain can process or handle.

Another characteristic shared by empaths is a great sense of intuition. They may get intense feelings when something is going wrong. Barrie Sueskind is a therapist in Los Angeles who specializes in relationships. According to Sueskind, "An empath's intuition can always identify whether or not someone is telling the truth." Aside from that, empaths struggle in huge groups due to their ability to perceive an excessive number of other people's emotions and moods. Empaths have the ability to absorb all energy, whether negative or positive. Other people rely on empaths to open up about their feelings since empaths have a difficult time not caring about others and want to help those who are struggling by absorbing their unpleasant emotions. As a result, empaths struggle to draw a line or set boundaries, despite the fact that they are a crucial aspect of every good connection.

Empaths typically seek refuge in peaceful settings surrounded by nature. They can relax and be at peace by not being among others and instead being in nature. Empaths find that sensing and feeling a wide range of emotions and energy drains them, so they recharge and refresh themselves in nature and solitude.

You might be shocked to learn that there are many varieties of empaths because each empath's experience and feelings are unique.

- **Emotional empath:** The most prevalent sort of empath is an emotional empath. Unlike intuitive empaths, they can experience the emotions of others as if they were their own, but only after they know what happened. If a buddy receives a gift that they enjoy, emotional empaths can rejoice with them.
- **Physical empath:** Physical empathy occurs when an empath is attuned to other people's physical cues and appears to absorb them into their own body. This happens even when someone is in pain.
- **Intuitive empath:** An intuitive empath can sense even the unsaid in order to comprehend what is going on around them or what someone is feeling.
- **Animal empath:** These empaths form a special relationship with animals or pets. They can converse with animals and comprehend what they desire. Because these empaths are nearly invariably animal lovers, animal maltreatment or violence is not an option.
- **Earth empath:** Earth empaths are sensitive to changes in our planet and solar system, as well as weather patterns. They can foresee natural disasters such as earthquakes.

- **Plant empath:** Plant empaths may sense the needs of plants and connect with them. These people are always the most knowledgeable about plants!
- **Dream empath:** These empaths have a strong ability to recall their dreams vividly. They can gain intuitive knowledge from their dreams, which they and others can benefit from.

Are You an Empath?

I've made a checklist for you to review that will assist you to figure out if you're an empath by nature. But don't panic if you don't recognize any of these characteristics in yourself; you could still be an empath. In addition, the next chapter will look at how you can learn to be an empath even if it isn't an inherent characteristic.

Check all that apply

You can feel other people's emotions along with them as well as have a deep understanding of their emotions.

Intimacy or closeness can be overwhelming for you.

You find it stressful to be in crowds.

You have a keen sense of intuition.

You find yourself drawn to nature and places without a lot of people.

You tend to avoid fights and conflicts.

People often come to you to talk about their problems.

You're extremely sensitive to sounds, smells, and sensations.

You find it difficult to set boundaries.

You perceive/see the world differently than others.

It's difficult for you to deal with an overload of emotions.

CHAPTER 2
HOW TO BECOME AN EMPATH?

BEING an empath is sometimes misunderstood as an intrinsic trait rather than something that can be gradually developed and mastered. With some practice and a short tutorial on how to become an empath, you'll be able to teach your subconscious the skill of empathic emotions. According to research, empathy is a taught attribute, with measurable empathic growth beginning as early as infancy. Although your current capacity to feel empathy beyond what is deemed normal is mostly controlled by your genetics and early experiences, the ordinary adult's mind appears to be flexible and capable of change. As a result, you can train your mind to think about things that aren't natural to you.

To begin, we must acknowledge that empathic and empathetic are not synonymous. Being empathetic is being able to understand and communicate another's feelings; but being an empath means being able to physically perceive another's feelings, joys, and miseries. Empaths don't merely acknowledge another person's suffering; they live through and feel it as if it were their own. Empaths can make the most of their abilities by understanding others and acting as a source of positive energy. A step-by-step guide on how to become an empath is provided below, which may assist you in focusing your energy on something meaningful.

Practicing active listening is the first step in becoming an empath. When starting a discussion, your natural instinct is to just listen. This implies that you take in the sound and evaluate it only to the degree where you can come up with a good response. Although this may not be a problem when discussing relatively unimportant topics, it may make the other person feel unheard when discussing more essential issues. You must adjust your emphasis from simply hearing to actively listening to the meaning behind the words expressed in these situations. To fully comprehend the speaker's narrative and point of view, you should clear your thoughts of any unnecessary distractions and focus entirely on their verbal and nonverbal signs. As you improve your listening skills, you will become more aware of other people's feelings and your intuitive abilities will grow.

Getting some alone time can help you improve your empathic abilities. Before you can truly comprehend and relate to other people's feelings and experiences, you must first thoroughly comprehend and relate to your own. A probable disagreement between your conscious and subconscious minds can cause a schism in your understanding of your emotions. If you are having negative thoughts and feelings about something or an incident that is preventing you from connecting with others on a deeper level, you must confront it. Understanding your own sentiments is the only way to know the significance behind other people's feelings.

On the road to becoming an empath, you'll need to learn to be more compassionate. You will be more empathic if it is easier for you to put yourself in other people's shoes. With time, your knowledge of others' sentiments will improve dramatically, and you will become more sensitive to their emotions. Humans are complex organisms with a tremendous deal of depth beneath the surface. You must focus your energy on diving deeper and breaking through the shallow and superficial layers.

We are inclined to acquire judgments about another person and their message based on our prejudices and prior beliefs when speaking with them. To be an empath, you must let go of the ideals and prejudices you've developed over the course of your life and see things from various perspectives separate from your own. Rather than categorizing individuals based on your predispositions, master seeing them for who they are: human beings.

Empathy can be enhanced by paying attention to your surroundings. Take care of everything in your environment—animals, plants, or people—whether it's alive or non-living. Spending time cultivating your relationship with nature can help you tap into your empathic senses. This can simply be accomplished by periodically checking in with those in your immediate vicinity or by feeding and caring for a stray animal. When you show kindness to the world, it returns the favor by satisfying your desire to become an empath. Take advantage of every opportunity you have to improve your connection to the world and the people and animals who live in it.

If you have a lot of money and privileges, one method to improve your empathic talents is to help those who are in difficult situations. It's a wonderful start to speak up for and assist underprivileged communities. Because we live in a capitalist system, donating to a charity is one of the most effective ways to help those in need. Being an empath is thus defined as taking action to aid others who are in need.

The human brain is capable of incredible feats. If you have a strong enough belief in something, it may truly come true. It's possible that pretending to be an empath will help you become one. This self-fulfilling prophecy is the outcome of your impact on your mind, as well as your mind's influence on you. Continuously behaving in an empathic manner will eventually turn you into one. Behaving more generously and compassionately should be your goal, and believing that doing so will enhance your talents can help you become an empath in the future.

According to studies, those who read fiction on a regular basis have a stronger capacity for empathy. By exercising the neurons involved in empathy, reading such stories increases neural systems. Immersing yourself in fiction and putting yourself in the shoes of a character makes it easier to do the same in real life.

CHAPTER 3
EMPATHS AND PSYCHIC ABILITIES

A PSYCHIC EMPATH is someone who is very sensitive to other people's emotions and sentiments. They're also acutely aware of their own internal emotional condition, which some may describe as finely tuned intuition or gut instinct. A psychic empath may look into the soul of another person. This can be a wonderful gift as well as a source of immense anguish if they get swamped by what they see. A psychic empath may also be able to sense more information than a normal person. People's feelings, ideas, aspirations, and sentiments can be included in ways that appear to be psychic powers—the capacity to perceive more information than the average individual can. This includes perceiving other realms' presences or energies. These could be interpreted as psychic powers or "vibes."

A psychic empath is someone who has a strong sense of empathy and understands others better than the average person. They have an instinctive desire to assist them in healing when they are harmed, which is something that happens frequently! They'll put in the effort to understand one another so that everyone feels recognized and valued.

Are you a Psychic Empath?

I've created another checklist for you to fill out. Are you a Psychic Empath? Let's find out!

Check all that may apply

You deeply feel other people's emotions but are also capable of healing them by absorbing some negative energy from them.

You are able to sense energies from different realms.

You can sense, and tune into other people's thoughts.

You may experience psychic-like visions.

You may be able to see through the veil between the living and the dead. Ghosts and spirits may be some of those things.

CHAPTER 4
EMPATHS AND HEALING

EMPATHS ARE enlightened souls who are incarnating in greater numbers on Earth to offer hope during this period of transformation. At present, there are more empaths on the planet than ever before. Empathy comes in a variety of forms. And as an empath, you're likely to experience varying levels of empathy at different points in your life. However, the majority of empaths have super abilities or traits. Agreeableness, optimism about human nature, a willingness to compromise, and concern for societal concord are among them.

Here are some of the most prominent super traits of empaths;

- **Extremely sensitive.** Noises, odors, and a lack of energy might be overwhelming.

- **Spiritually attuned.** Feel as if you're connected to a greater power.
- **Attuned to the moods of others.** Take into account other people's feelings,
- **Introverted.** Prefer one-on-one or small-group interactions. If you're outgoing, you might want to limit how much time you spend in a crowd or at a party.
- **Intuitive.** Can tell when things aren't right.
- **When it comes to intimate relationships, easily overwhelmed.** It's tough to have too much closeness.
- **Energy vampires' prey.** Egotists, drama queens, and persistent loudmouths can entrap you.
- **Fueled by nature.** Seek solace in the natural world.
- **Big hearts.** Good listeners often give too much. Take on the agony of others to relieve it, but then you feel depleted.

These super traits can often be used to heal one's own self or heal others. There are a number of ways in which an empath can transform these traits into superpowers. Below are a few examples:

- **Recognize your empathic nature.**
  Compassion is your purpose if you're an empath. Since birth, you've been programmed to be the planet's light anchor. The first step toward allowing your inner light to shine is acknowledging that you came here to accomplish this.
- **Have faith in your instincts.** You are extremely sensitive as an empath. Learning to trust yourself and the information you receive will help you avoid energy vampires and discover positive, healthy connections, whether you can read people's minds, see psychic visions, pick up on odors, or detect a feeling in your stomach. You can use these hunches to help others find loving relationships and heal from toxic ones as well.
- **Playing the victim isn't a good idea.**
  Empaths frequently lack self-esteem. Your urge to be adored can eventually morph into a victim mindset. This is frequent in spiritual partnerships when the guru ends up taking all of the resources while the devotees lose their self-esteem, money, and other resources. For the betterment of yourself and others, you must remain empowered.

EMPATH & PSYCHIC ABILITIES: 29

- **Define your boundaries.** Once you've figured out who your energy vampires are, put a time restriction on how much time you spend with them. Take note of how you feel while with them and how you feel thereafter. You'll soon be able to walk away for good and reclaim your valuable energy. You'll also have a lot more free time to do something you enjoy.
- **Meditation.** Empaths require downtime to reenergize. Empaths can benefit from meditation, which takes only a few moments. When you're experiencing sensory overload, this is a fantastic way to reclaim your power. You don't have to sit to meditate, though. Spend time in nature or visualize yourself in a safe bubble where only light can pass through but dark energy cannot. Repeat this process multiple times a day.
- **Breathing.** Create a breathing practice in which you simply sit and breathe consciously. Consider the words "clarity" and "strength" while you inhale. Consider breathing out bad energy as you exhale. "I am breathing in strength," you can even say. "I'm exhaling my anxiety and negativity." Do

this multiple times a day to relieve any stress that has built up in your body.

- **Negative energy must be transformed.** As empaths, we pick up a lot of negative energy from the people around us. Use techniques to convert negative energy in real time. Bring plants into your workstation, for example, to assist absorb negative energy. Crystals, which are natural energy modulators, are another option. Surround yourself with things that are beautiful. In a difficult scenario, try to communicate positively. When feasible, find the comedy in a situation to help shift negative energy. Another thing you can do to boost your positive energy is to begin each day with gratitude mantras.
- **Take care of yourself.** Your life's goal as an empath is to look after you. It's the only thing you're supposed to do! Self-empathy is the ability to listen to one's own ideas and emotions. Every day, set aside some time to recognize your emotions and accept your sensitivities. Recognize that you can be sensitive while also being strong. Every time you follow your instincts or accomplish something that makes you happier, stronger, or healthier, give yourself a pat on the back.

Remember that when you reach your greatest potential, you have the power to change the lives of others.

Empaths and Crystal Healing

Being an empath or an HSP means you're continuously absorbing other people's energies and feelings. You have a hard time distinguishing your own ideas and feelings from those of others. This frequently results in befuddlement, restlessness, and a heaviness in the aura. The forces that are continually whirling around you overwhelm you. You may put out the wrong message or sign if you don't manage it effectively, and you may draw the interest of individuals who are accustomed to emptying or pouring their emotional energy, problems, and troubles on you.

To be an empath, on the other hand, isn't all awful. The ability to empathize with others is a skill that will enable you to assist others. Energy healers, psychics, and spiritual seekers are all known for their high sensitivity. To be able to both help others and yourself overcome problems, establishing explicit emotional, cognitive, and energetic boundaries with others is crucial, and this is where empathic crystals may help.

Crystals can be helpful allies for empaths. Finding folks who understand where you're coming from might be difficult at times. However, because crystals are silent helpers, you won't have to worry about causing extra drama or talking about your difficulties if you utilize healing and protection crystals. They don't judge you if you have unresolved issues or baggage because they work to help you get rid of it. They do everything without grumbling, and they offer you unconditional love and support anytime you need it. They are energy allies who unconditionally assist you in order to relieve your emotional and energetic tension. They have the ability to brighten your life and assist you in living it the way you choose.

Section 7 of this book discusses crystal healing in detail, but here is a list of a few crystals that assist empaths to reach their full potential.

Hematite

Hematite is an excellent stone to use to calm your emotions and keep you grounded. It surrounds you in a protective barrier, shielding you from undesired and unwanted vibrations. It aids you in avoiding those who deplete your energy for their own wants and demands. This stone helps you revive your enthusiasm for life. It possesses greater powers that can assist you in finding answers to a variety of questions.

Amethyst

Amethyst is known to be one of the most potent stones on the planet. It's always a good idea to use it when doing any kind of energy work. This is because it is a spiritual growth stone that connects the physical body to the spiritual world through the head chakra. Amethyst jewelry can also aid in the transformation of negative energy into positive.

Amethyst is a crystal that immediately helps you feel lighter. It boosts your psychic abilities while also providing psychic protection. It shields you from negative energies while attracting favorable ones. It awakens the upper chakras' powers and removes the evil eye, negative energy, and curses.

Black Tourmaline

Black tourmaline is regarded as one of the most effective empathic defense crystals. It assists in keeping negative energies away so you won't have to consume them. Empaths are quite good at absorbing electromagnetic frequencies from their surroundings, leaving them susceptible and exposed.

This stone protects you from anything and everything that has a powerful effect or emits electromagnetic pollutants. It takes negative energy and stores it inside itself. It further protects you from telepathic attacks of any type. It resists negative energy and shields you from nasty people by stopping them from passing their bad energy to you. This gemstone can be carried or worn as a talisman, but it can also be used as a protective amulet.

You can actually put bits of tourmaline all over your house to keep vile people and feelings away. Shamans used black tourmaline to fight off bad spirits in earlier civilizations.

Rose Quartz

Rose Quartz is often regarded as the most "potent stone for the heart," and it can assist empaths in letting go of any grief or pain that is driving the heart chakra to become obstructed. It aids in the purification and reawakening of the heart. It's also quite useful when dealing with harmful individuals and circumstances. It's a benevolent gem with a soft but potent vibration. Adding to that, it aids in the release of past life challenges and traumas. It keeps you from absorbing other people's energies and increases your charisma by emitting compassion everywhere around you.

Lapis Lazuli

Another amazing crystal for empaths is the magical brilliance that is lapis lazuli. This is a brave crystal that gives you the uncompromising ability to dig deep within yourself and listen to your own inner wisdom. Being an empath can put you off your game from time to time. It can be difficult to discover your unique perspective in the midst of the crowd when we are easily influenced by others' whims and viewpoints. Lapis lazuli balances your throat chakra and encourages you to stand up in a variety of ways without hesitation.

Moonstone

Moonstone is a magnificent therapeutic stone for driving the darkness away, with its white color and feminine vitality. Moonstone, a crystal of self-improvement and fortitude, keeps emotions mild and stable. This gleaming white relic is a traveler's stone that protects individuals who travel by road. Moonstone can improve intuition and offer good fortune to empaths, warding off negative vibes and keeping them connected to the divine light.

Black Kyanite

Black kyanite defends your energy from those who feed off of your positivism and takes care of your harmful ties. This stone makes you think about what's holding you back. You may emit energy that you don't need once you've determined which energy is yours and which has simply been glued to you. This stone integrates your energy field and interacts with all of your chakras.

Citrine

Citrine is among the finest crystals for eliminating toxic barriers and increasing the energy centers connection. Self-will, personal strength, creative genius, and achieving your greatest wishes are all themes that this gold crystal explores. Citrine is drenched in spectacular healing and is ever-ready to lift you up and relieve any distress you may be experiencing. Citrine will spread its beams and bring summer joys back to empaths who are sick of the dark cloud haunting them.

Fluorite

Just a glimpse at the fluorite crystal is sufficient to lift your spirits and put you in a good mood. Fluorite is renowned for delving into lower frequencies that aid you in standing tall. This stone will make the empath feel safe and comfortable and have them be ready to investigate what's going on deep inside them. This sense of stability is essential for empaths to feel as though they can continue on whilst remaining strong.

Clear Quartz

Clear quartz emits pristine energy, making it an excellent crystal for empaths looking to replace pessimism with something a little more uplifting. Clear quartz's ability to enhance energy is one of its most powerful properties. When used in conjunction with other healing gems, it amplifies their effectiveness. That isn't to suggest that clear quartz can't be used on its alone; it can help with relaxation, emotional balance, and reducing darker thoughts inherited from others.

Lepidolite

Lepidolite is among the most relaxing and balanced stones available. This crystal is regarded as the serenity crystal and a gemstone of smooth transition because of its positive vibes. Lepidolite is very effective at assisting individuals who are experiencing psychological overload. Lepidolite might assist you in getting back on course whenever you are feeling overwhelmed. It also lessens the effects of electromagnetic fields and clears the pathways between the heart and the rest of the body.

How can Empaths Use These Crystals for Healing?

For millennia, crystals have been utilized to manipulate energies in order to access the chakra capabilities of the human body. You can use the healing crystals' abilities for your own good by performing strong rituals such as meditation, visualization, cleansings, amulets, and energy grids.

Meditation

Here are some ways in which you can meditate with crystals:

1. Crystals should be placed on your chakras. Chakras are known to be a set of energy centers on the body that symbolize many aspects of the biological and metaphysical self. If your desire for crystal meditation is healing, focusing on the chakra that corresponds to your meditation objective while using a suitable stone is perfect.
2. Take the crystals in your hands and embrace them. Holding crystals in your palm and clearing your mind can be enough to help you meditate. Holding a crystal in your hand while meditating allows you to naturally exchange energies and frequencies with the stone, allowing you to experience its benefits.

3. Make a crystal energy field using your hands. Some people prefer not to have stones touch their bodies during meditation, in which case building a crystal circle might be a useful technique to interact with crystal vibration without physical contact. It is suggested that you make a circle with the stones to protect yourself. To wrap oneself in crystal energy, arrange one crystal in front, one behind, and one on each side of you. You can meditate with one or more types of crystals, but you must engage with them in order to connect yourself with their strong frequencies.

Visualizations

You can do two types of visualizations, both of which are highly advocated for empaths.

The Initial Visualization

The first one is performed when you wake up in the morning, and the latter is conducted before you go to sleep at night. Sit peacefully, arms spread, and take deep breaths. Consider a massive pair of scissors severing any negative energetic bonds and ties. This helps you to merge with your energy release.

The Following Visualization

The second type of visualization is used to prepare your head for a possibly stressful circumstance. Empaths will benefit from this since it allows them to get in the appropriate mindset before entering a space or walking into a situation. For this one, you must sit calmly in a tranquil spot and take prolonged, deep breaths. Imagine a gigantic dome growing around you once you've found your center. This enormous bubble serves as a safety shield for you. Recite a mantra that assures you that you will be secure and guarded. You're prepared to end the visualization technique when you believe that this defensive barrier is powerful enough to withstand the harmful energies of the day.

Cleansings

After using your crystals, it is absolutely necessary to cleanse them. This can be done using sage. Sage is a mystical plant that has a wide range of medicinal benefits. It's thought that smudging your stone would clear out any unwanted frequencies and recover its natural vitality.

Alleviate the evil and burdensome forces that have descended upon you by cleansing your environment with sage. It will keep negative energy from darkening your thoughts and environment. Sage once or twice a day, or as needed. Allow the cleansing smoke to drift into the most active parts of your room. Keep an eye out for windows, entrances, and closets.

This technique will also help you clear your psychological palette and establish healthy spiritual parameters within your aura. You will improve your view and enable yourself to regulate your moods if you take these precautions to safeguard yourself. When you're feeling physically or mentally drained, using cleansed crystals might help you notice the energy around you. It significantly minimizes your energy use. When you're cursed or sick, your supernatural aura dissipates as well. Use cleansed crystals for heightened powers to ensure that your empathic capabilities remain strong.

Amulets

An amulet is a unique talisman that is worn for protection and safety. Crystal structures form when particular gemstones and minerals form, concentrating their strength to shield and defend you. Amulets are protective gems that are frequently worn or carried. Amulets can only be made with certain gemstones.

Talismans and crystal amulets are simple to include in your daily life. Several familiar stones, such as amethyst, hematite, and sapphire, can be obtained from jewelers, while specialty merchants and artisan jewelers may carry rarer types. Holistic and metaphysical stores frequently stock crystal jewelry. If you like, you can purchase a variety of crystal beads as well as other elements to make your own jewelry. If you can't or don't want to wear jewelry, gemstones could be kept in a pocket or backpack or placed out of sight in your blouse or shoe pit.

All items utilized in the creation of amulets and talismans must be purified before usage, just like any other crystal craft. The thing is subsequently charged with intention when it has been picked or constructed. This can be accomplished in a variety of ways, depending on your personal beliefs and spiritual path, and can range from intricate rituals to basic prayer or meditation.

Energy Grids

A crystal grid is just a symmetric layout of crystals intended to boost the energy of said crystals. They assist in storing and managing energy in the same way that an electrical grid does. Holy geometric motifs such as the Seed of Life or Metatron's Cube are used as guides for stone placement in conventional crystal grid designs. The designs on the crystal lattice can be different. The most important thing is to understand how to energize crystals with intentions and how to use the grid to support your psychic practice.

A crystal grid can assist you in achieving your goals or establishing the aura of a room. For your normal healing activities or divine rituals, you can use particular crystal grids. These grids assist you in channeling, focusing, and directing energy. Even if you're not convinced of stone healing's effectiveness, crystal grids can serve as lovely mementos of your aspirations. They're periodic affirmations that can help you become more self-aware, accountable, and motivated to take more deliberate activities for protracted growth and success.

An empath who follows all these healing tips and tricks will definitely save themselves a lot of heartache and, in fact, be able to maximize their potential as a psychic. Continue reading further to learn more about psychic abilities and how to use them properly.

PART TWO
PSYCHIC ABILITIES

CHAPTER 5
BASICS

WE'LL TALK about psychic abilities, clairvoyance, telepathy, and more in this section of the book. To begin, we must first identify psychic abilities and the circumstances surrounding their emergence.

Psychic powers have survived and thrived in modern society, despite their origins in archaic times. Believers in abilities transcending natural human senses have a long history. A number of the mystics believed that they could make precise forecasts about a variety of things by using their intuition or visions that contained impending revelations. These persons, known as seers, took on important roles such as clergy, advisers, and jurors.

As a result, we can observe that as the modern generation arose, spirituality stayed at its peak, and mystical ideas became a significant element of human culture. This revolution dismantled rigid old religious ideas and substituted them with mystical enlightenment.

In today's society, a psychic is defined as an individual who retains extrasensory perception, or the ability to discern things not evident to the human eye using normal senses. These persons with psychic abilities were considered to possess a sixth sense that allowed them to see and experience things that regular folk couldn't. Spiritual readers offer advice on numerous elements of life, such as romance, marriage, profession, wealth, and so on, to those who want their assistance.

Psychic talents are widely assumed to be inherent. They are present in everyone to some extent. Some individuals are born with a particular sort of expertise, while others are gifted with another. Although some capabilities are innate, they can be strengthened and improved with significant practice. Regardless of the fact that becoming a psychic is within anyone's grasp, we must remember to exercise prudence and caution when wielding these abilities, since tremendous power comes with massive responsibility.

We can now move on to briefly outlining the various categories of heightened sensory capabilities since we've covered the basics of their origin and significance.

Clairvoyance is amongst the most well-known psychic skills, if not the most well-known. It is also the most common sort of psychic talent. An obvious distinguishing quality of this is exceptional skill or insight into forthcoming events while possessing no previous experience in regard to the subject. Their perception appears to come from a supernatural or mysterious source. Although foretelling the future is an important aspect of clairvoyance, it is not the only one. Whether it's former occurrences or incidents that are far outside the realm of realism, clairvoyance is present in all of them. Clairvoyance makes use of the third eye, sometimes known as the mind's eye, to obtain vital knowledge that can help mankind in a variety of ways, including solving crimes, foreseeing disasters, and lots more.

There are several typical clairvoyant characteristics that can help you figure out how attuned you are to your true self. Lucid dreams, visions, unusually strong senses, and plenty more are among them. Conversely, because each individual's uniqueness influences what they experience, stereotyping clairvoyant encounters may be much too simplified. Our abilities and how our bodies react to them are shaped and molded by the unique essence that constitutes the fiber of our existence.

Continuing ahead, telepathy is a type of heightened sensory perception and a remarkable psychic gift. It is defined as the exchange of one person's ideas or feelings to another without the use of standard channels of communication. Dreams were thought to be the primary basis of telepathy in medieval societies. As time went on, these perspectives evolved, and senses that were not subject to physical laws came to be regarded as the source of the capacity to perceive others' thoughts. All existence comes from a metaphysical source, and we are all connected in some manner; this is the foundation of telepathic faith.

After you are calm and relaxed, your telepathic talents are substantially strengthened. The absorption and distribution of telepathic signals are considerably more receptive by relaxing your mind and body. The practice of telepathy is aided by the elimination of unnecessary thoughts from our minds, which can be disruptive. Upon cleansing your mind of undesirable distractions, you will be free to use the telepathic transmission to send and receive messages.

If the information intended to be transmitted has been conveyed, the mind's eye detects it. You might visualize the information you acquired if you were the receiver of the message.

I've made a checklist for you to determine whether or not you have psychic abilities!

Mark all that apply

You see auras. Auras aren't definitive colors around people but you may see different tints surrounding people.

You have strong gut feelings.

You may feel magnetized toward a specific direction.

You often predict future events. it doesn't have to be an exact prediction, it can be a general one too.

You have vivid dreams. Your dreams feel too real, and things you dream about often end up happening in real life.

You have extremely sharp senses. Better known as extrasensory perception, you may sense others' thoughts and feelings.

You're extremely empathetic or an "empath." You may find it very easy to put yourself in other people's shoes. So much so that you feel their pain with them.

You may find yourself getting déjà vu often.

CHAPTER 6
TELEPATHY

TELEPATHY IS a sort of extrasensory perception that involves the immediate transfer of a thought from one individual (sender) to another (receiver) without the need for standard physical communication channels. The term telepathy was coined in 1882 by Frederic W. H. Myers, a representative of the Association for Psychical Exploration. The terminology has stayed more popular than its former name: thought-transference.

If you've ever studied a book regarding psychic powers, you might be startled to learn that telepathy has a lot of scientific support. Washington Irving Bishop, a prominent "thought-reader" in the late 1800s, was noted for his capability to use heightened sensory perception to decipher other individuals' thoughts. His practice became so well-known that he was analyzed by a team of scientists and psychologists. Items would be buried beneath a table throughout these studies, and Bishop was asked to locate the areas where the said items were placed. The response would be presented to a person or "assistant," and Bishop would grasp their palms or wrists before responding. He was able to supply all of the correct answers.

Bishop professed to having no mystical powers, instead he relied on his enhanced awareness of sensory perception as well as people's body signals to conduct telepathy. As a result, this book does not argue that telepathy or psychic capabilities are mystical or elements of sorcery, but instead abilities that are well within human capacity. For this reason, we suppose that a small number of people are susceptible to telepathy, and you may be one of those individuals! Telepathy was seen by Sigmund Freud, a well-known neurologist and psychologist, as an intrinsic human talent that was repressed during evolution. We think there really are methods to bring back those talents.

Continue reading further to learn more about telepathy and review a checklist that will reveal whether you hone psychic abilities!

TYPES OF TELEPATHY

Superconscious Telepathy: This sort of telepathy involves accessing the superconscious, or ultimate level of awareness. This is usually done for the sake of personal development and wellness. Superconscious telepathy allows people to access and learn from the collective wisdom that humans have accumulated over time. In layman's terms, it's the process of improving oneself by tapping into the collective conscience of those around you.

Retro Cognitive, Precognitive, and Intuitive Telepathy: The communication of information regarding a person's past, future, or current mental state to another person is referred to as this type of telepathy. Consider putting a person's entire life and memories on a USB drive, then inserting that drive into another human and transferring all of the data to the new host. This is essentially retro cognitive, precognitive, and intuitive telepathy.

Latent Telepathy: This was originally known as "Deferred Telepathy," and it is the transfer of thoughts from one person to another, with the exception of an observable time lag. It takes a certain amount of time for information to reach the intended recipient.

Emotive Telepathy: Kinesthetic perceptions are communicated through changed states, according to this category of telepathy. Emotional transfer or remote influence are other terms for it

Dream Telepathy: Dream telepathy is the capacity to communicate with another person telepathically while dreaming. Dream communication is very different than talking to someone in person or over the internet. When we communicate through dreams, we are in a vulnerable yet emancipated position. This is the kind of connection that leads us beyond the ego or superego's limitations. Unfortunately, few people remember these dream talks, and they occur more frequently than we might imagine.

Dream telepathy has been studied, and you'd be shocked how much proof they've gathered! In a particular experiment, one person acted as a "transmitter" and another as a "receiver" who was asleep and had electrodes attached to their brain to detect REM sleep. Dream telepathy is more likely to occur during the REM state of sleep, which is when people have the most vivid dreams. The transmitter starts to focus on a specific image when the recording device detects a new REM stage. The image is then telepathically transferred into the sleeper's dream by them.

Here's a fun fact: If you don't know what a twin flame is, you should read the next few sentences carefully because we'll mention it several times throughout the book. A twin flame is a concept in which one soul is incarnated in two bodies. Although people seldom meet or reconcile with their twin flame, you may have met them in your dreams. Dream telepathy is a typical way for twin flames to communicate. It might even make your search for them go more smoothly.

Twin Telepathy: Twin telepathy is a mystical or, given recent evidence, a scientific phenomenon in which one twin can analyze the other's thoughts, sentiments, or emotions without the other twin saying anything. Telepathy allows a twin to know what the other twin is thinking or feeling even when they are not in the same room. For the two, it acts as a sixth sense.

Below are some twin telepathy stories. These are stories given by the twins themselves and uploaded to the *Buzzfeed* website. These accounts will make you doubt everything you've heard about twins.

1. **The twins' nightmare:** The twins tell of a dream in which they both saw the same neighborhood cousins die. They saw the

same sights, and although they rarely remember their dreams, they both remembered this one.

2. **Sharing near-death experiences:** One twin recounts his brother's night out with his mates as a near-death experience. The twin didn't feel at ease for some reason. All night long, he was tossing and turning, seeing flashes of police cars and sirens. A police call prompted their mother to hurry out of the house a few moments later. The other twin was speechless and in a state of astonishment. He confessed the next day that a car had attempted to run them over!

3. **The cheated cheaters:** Two twins were suspected of cheating on a test by writing the same essay on the same day. Each word was identical, but the twins had not discussed anything and were not seated in the same classroom. Furthermore, they were just in fourth grade and clearly incapable of devising any major cheating conspiracy. A few years later, while participating in athletics, one of the twins injured his collarbone. The second twin, who was at home at the time, began to complain of a strong discomfort in his chest.

4. **Seizure detector:** When these twins were younger, one of them would experience seizures in the middle of the night while the other slept. On the nights when one of the twins had seizures, the other would wake up with strange tunnel vision. The room would gradually lighten before becoming darker for this twin. It became a sign that her sister was having seizures. She would rush to her parents and inform them of the seizures so that they could be present when they occurred. If this doesn't blow your mind, I don't know what will!

5. **The heartache:** This is a story about a twin's mother and aunt, who were also twins. This girl's mother was in the shower when she began to experience strange chest pains.

She felt as if she was being sucked out of her life. She received a phone call moments later informing her that her sister was suffering from life-threatening heart complications.

Signs that you may have telepathic abilities!

Check all boxes that apply

You share the same views as your friends or family members.

You have a knack of saying exactly what other people are thinking.

You're good at assisting people who can't find the words to articulate what they want to convey.

You're a natural when it comes to nonverbal communication.

You have a solid sense of what newborns require.

You have a level of empathy for others that few people possess.

It is simple for you to persuade or influence others about your point of view.

When someone is speaking to you or telling a lie, you read between the lines.

"I was just thinking that," is a typical expression used by you.

CHAPTER 7
CLAIRVOYANCE

MANY OF US are capable of making informed decisions based on prior information. Clairvoyants are those who have the ability to foretell the future without having any prior information or connection to the matter at hand. The information comes from a divine source or might be attributed to an individual's intrinsic skills to see into the future using mystical methods.

The term "clairvoyance" is of French origin and is derived from a combination of two words that mean "clear" and "seeing." When clairvoyance comes up in conversation, it's frequently associated with foreseeing the future. This isn't completely accurate. Clairvoyance is much more than a woman in a crystal ball giving you your fortune. Clairvoyants are often endowed with abilities such as precognition, retrocognition, or even remote seeing, which is the perception of current events taking place outside of the normal realms of time and space.

Other Types of Clairvoyant Abilities

- Clairaudience: the ability to hear sounds that are not normally audible.
- Clairsentience: the ability to sense and understand the energies and feelings of not only people but also animals and things.
- Claircognizance: the ability to detect when someone obtains critical information.
- Clairsalience: the ability to smell energies.
- Clairgustance: the rarest ability to be able to taste energies.

SOME NOTABLE CLAIRVOYANTS AND THEIR ACCURATE PREDICTIONS

Nostradamus

Nostradamus was a well-known clairvoyant in the 16th century. He was known for making very specific future forecasts. The following is a list of some of his predictions that came true:

- The Great Fire of London

- Horrors of the French Revolution
- Napoleon's conquests
- Hitler's rule in Germany
- Catastrophes caused by WWI and WWII
- Atomic bombing of Hiroshima and Nagasaki
- Princess Diana's death
- September 11 attacks

Abraham Lincoln

Abraham Lincoln was reputed to be a clairvoyant who foretold his own death. While some may argue that it was just a coincidence, many numerous psychics disagree. It's difficult to be a mere prediction based on the details of his story! He told his wife the day before he was shot:

"He was woken up by the sound of crying and went into the East Room of the White House, where a casket was laid open. There was a throng of mourners as well as several men guarding the casket. When he asked who was in the casket, one of the soldiers told him that it was the President, who had been killed by an assassin."

Anne Moberly and Eleanor Jourdain

Anne Moberly and Eleanor Jourdain, two scholars, were touring the Palace of Versailles when they became disoriented and stated that a profound gloom settled upon them. They came across several personalities from over a century ago, such as the Comte de Vaudreuil and Marie Antoinette, before making their way out. Some call it time travel, while others call it clairvoyant retrocognition.

CHAPTER 8
PARAPSYCHOLOGY & OTHER RESEARCH

PARAPSYCHOLOGY

Parapsychology is a discipline of psychology that focuses on evaluating paranormal psychological evidence in areas such as clairvoyance, telepathy, and other abilities. It is the study of a supernatural phenomenon that gives rationale to psychic powers that cannot be explained by normal sensory abilities. Parapsychology is primarily concerned with investigating experiences that defy universal laws.

FAMOUS PARAPSYCHOLOGISTS AND THEIR RESEARCH

Marquis de Puységur

Franz Anton Mesmer, a German physicist, promoted the hypothesis of animal magnetism, which supported his theory that life forms are influenced by unknown energies. The thoughts and structure put out by Mesmer were changed by Marquis de Puységur, a protégé of Mesmer. He came across an unusual occurrence that he dubbed "manufactured somnambulism," a mental state that occurs between sleep and alertness. According to this, people may experience "lucidity" regarding matters that are outside the scope of regular awareness, leading to a trance-like state. In this context, the terms lucidity and clairvoyance are interchangeable. As time went on, a new perspective on the human psyche emerged, with people being able to access a suppressed self through hypnosis. This self would store information about the person and the universe that went beyond the limits of human perception.

William Gregory

William Gregory, a Scottish physician and chemist, had also been fascinated by mesmerism. In his book *Letters to a Candid Inquirer, on Animal Magnetism*, he described what has been defined as "traveling clairvoyance." The presence of cases where an entranced subject was sent to a remote area and questioned about their surroundings was noted by him. Although the individuals under observation did not always express sensations of physically leaving the body, there was typically awareness of being present in an unfamiliar environment. Details of places, objects, and people were correctly identified by these individuals let alone as suitably as a person present in those situations, which would be implausible under ordinary circumstances.

Rudolf Tischner

Rudolf Tischner was a parapsychologist and ophthalmologist from Germany who is most known for his parapsychology research. He wrote various articles and books on telekinesis, telepathy, spirituality, and other topics, among others. He intended to develop a German equivalent, influenced by the British Society for Psychical Research. One of his most important contributions to the study of parapsychology was his research on clairvoyance. Experiments included people determining the contents of opaque envelopes containing writing or sketches with no prior knowledge of the envelopes' composition. Tischner detected senses beyond what science could account for in clairvoyance and telepathy and invented the term "extrasensory perception" to describe them.

Extrasensory Perception/Sixth Sense

As you may be aware, parapsychology is primarily concerned with the study of supernatural powers, with extrasensory perception (ESP) serving as the basis for these. ESP sometimes known as the sixth sense, refers to information gained through means other than the senses or inferred from prior experience. It is distinct from recognized sensory processes and belongs to the same category as clairvoyance, telepathy, and other psychic talents. This supernatural awareness of events outside of our five senses exposes details about people, objects, or events that would otherwise be unknown. Since the late 1800s, scientists have been researching the hypothesis of ESP. Card guessing tests have been the most prevalent sort of experiment used to prove the presence of ESP.

The ganzfeld experiment was used to test the ESP hypothesis, which places an individual, the sender, in a separate area to exclude the possibility of nonverbal communication. A computer selects an image or video at random from a large collection. The other participant, the receiver, is sitting comfortably in a separate area. Outside noise is reduced, and participants are placed in a calming dream-like state of consciousness. The transmitter claims responsibility for focusing on the target and transmitting it to the listener mentally. Throughout this time, a constant description of any visualization or observation made by the receiver is provided. The receiver is only directed to choose the target among four stimuli delivered at the end of the session, three of which are decoys. The results of these experiments were extremely positive. A 35% accuracy grade was observed in a sample of 28 tests done between 1974 and 1981. Although this may not appear to be a large number, it is a considerable estimate that is exceedingly unlikely to be justified by chance or luck.

Joseph Banks Rhine's Research on ESP

Joseph Banks Rhine, the creator of parapsychology, conducted a particularly well-known investigation in the field. He adopted the term "extrasensory perception" while researching the cognitive processes that underpin telepathy and clairvoyance. Rhine conducted his studies on a group of students who volunteered to be the subjects of his research. One of his first notable topics was Adam Linzmayer. Linzmayer excelled in the Zener card (cards used to perform tests as evidence for clairvoyance and ESP) tests administered by Rhine in 1931, scoring 100% on the two brief tests given to him. Linzmayer, by chance, got 39.6% of his first long test right, even though the probability of getting it right was only 20%, putting him well outside the realm of chance.

As a result, Rhine included Hubert Pearce as a volunteer in his experiments. Pearce averaged 40% higher than Linzmayer's total score, which was 20% higher than chance. Pearce was then included in what is undoubtedly Rhine's most well-known series of tests. Inside a parapsychology laboratory 100 yards away from where Pearce was stationed, Rhine's research assistant reorganized and logged the sequence of the Zener cards. The results of these trials showed Pearce's accurate estimates to be dramatically above chance, implying that parapsychology and the existence of a higher sense exist.

Psychokinesis was simplified and researched in a lab environment with controls to observe the effect of the stimuli, since it was a topic he was very interested in. The goal of this study was to see how much an individual might influence the outcome of tossed dice. Rhine collaborated on a paper with his colleagues after completing his investigation, reviewing the information acquired on clairvoyance and telepathy. His contributions to parapsychology are notable, and his work continues to be important in understanding mental capacities that are outside of the usual.

Now let's find out whether you're telepathic!

Check all that may apply

You experience similar thoughts at the same time as people you are close to.

You voice what others seem to be thinking.

You often help those who can't find words to describe what they're feeling.

You are excellent at nonverbal communication.

You have strong instincts about children, especially babies.

You deeply understand people in a way that others often don't.

You easily persuade others to see things from your perspective.

You can easily spot liars.

You feel the emotions and thoughts of loved ones who live in different cities or countries.

PART THREE
INTUITION

CHAPTER 9
WHAT IS INTUITION?

HAVE you ever felt negative energy around yourself, but you were not quite sure as to why you were experiencing it? Have you ever gotten a bad vibe from someone but suppressed that feeling beneath the layers of logic?

If you asked an individual what they think intuition is, their answer would be, "a person's gut feeling." In reality, intuition is much more than that. It is an individual's innate ability to get in touch with a deeper part of themselves. Unlike mathematics, intuition is not something that can be proven by numbers; thus, everyone has their own opinion as to what it is. Countless people acknowledge it while others simply dismiss such feelings as "coincidence."

Human beings need both reason and intuition to make an informed decision. Unfortunately, today's society has convinced us that intuition is not a reliable guidance tool while making a decision. In fact, what distinguishes humans from animals is our ability to reason. Intuitive individuals have a sense of vision, and they know how to effectively move toward that vision. Some people may feel a strong intuitive urge while it may be difficult for others to interpret what they are feeling. Those are the people who use conscious thought and logic while thinking.

Intuition can come in different forms. At times, intuitive information may manifest as a vague or misty sensation. At other times, it may hit you over the head. Intuition can sometimes be so intense that you can physically feel it. Some people describe this as a "sinking feeling" in their chest or stomach. Dreams can also be a way of your intuition trying to communicate with you. Every person has an intuitive ability but what separates us from others is how we use that ability.

People often confuse intuition with psychic abilities. However, the latter is quite different. Many individuals believe that developing psychic abilities requires voodoo, witchcraft, or a belief in the otherworldly. That, however, is not a true representation of the situation. Psychic ability is mostly based on trust in the mind's power and the ability to control one's own destiny. It's about a never-ending and unwavering search for truth using your own intuition and self-guidance system. It is the capacity to know the unknowable on an extremely deep emotional, physical, and spiritual level. It is an extension of intuition.

The key difference lies between the amount of information that a psychic person can interpret. Both work with the information we are not aware of on a conscious level. However, psychics possess a more powerful source of insight consistently. They are able to receive images and impressions from the mind in a symbolic or literal form that they interpret.

Normally, psychic abilities are developed during childhood. These gifts are either passed down or are a result of our surroundings. As children, we notice more, see more, hear more, and feel more. These are basic survival instincts that enable us to safely move through the world. But as we mature, we are told to stop being so sensitive, that ghosts aren't real, and that pain is always physical. Through this conditioning, we start to believe that emotions and intuition are antithetical to science and reason. We suppress our gifts, sneer at clairvoyants, and accept the full extent of reality.

Here's a checklist to see whether you have a keen intuition.

Check all that may apply

You are acutely aware of everyone's feelings.

Your dreams are vivid.

You have a keen eye for detail.

Thoughts appear out of nowhere in your head.

You're bombarded with stimuli from all sides.

You have a persistent ailment that doctors are unable to treat.

You're susceptible to becoming addicted.

You sense a unique affinity to nature.

Synchronicity follows you around.

CHAPTER 10
HOW TO AWAKEN YOUR INTUITION

THERE ARE a number of ways in which you can enrich and essentially awaken your intuition. To find out how you, as an average individual, can become more intuitive, keep on reading!

Meditation

We all are equipped with intuition and there are some ways to awaken it.

One of the most effective ways to do this is through meditation. Meditation isn't about becoming a better or a changed person but is about getting a healthy sense of perspective. It is a way to eliminate all the external distractions and focus on internal experiences. It can help us find a sense of peace and inner harmony, as well as deal with the stresses of daily life. Meditation is applicable to people of all faiths and cultures. It's less about what religion we follow and more about becoming more conscious, focused, and calm; more aware of our thoughts, speech, and actions; and more aware of how our decisions influence others. There are several different types of meditation.

Spiritual Meditation

Spiritual meditation is a transformative experience that brings you to the core of your being. You, as your true self, are devoid of any preconceived notions about yourself up to that point in time. You will feel joy and calm as a result of this exercise. Your being is warmed by a feeling of love and brightness. Spiritual meditation helps your body release all the stress and relaxes your nervous system. It helps you realize your true self and empowers you.

This kind of meditation involves five steps. The first is to find a comfortable and peaceful place to sit in. It is important that the place you choose is quiet because this kind of meditation can easily be disrupted by noise. Sit straight in a chair and close your eyes. The second step is to relax and allow the meditation to run its course in a natural way. You should remain a passive observer, allowing the process to unfold naturally. Do not be concerned about the outcome or about getting it right. Allow things to take their natural course. In today's world, everything is fed to us through social media. Our mind is always occupied. The third step is to calm our minds and free ourselves from all worldly matters. We are always bombarded by thoughts which makes it hard for us to concentrate even while meditating. The difficulty lies in refusing to respond to such thoughts and allowing them to exert influence over you. Allow thoughts to come to you naturally but resist the desire to react to them. Allow them to drift away so you could return to your meditation. The next step is to choose a prayer in your brain as you sit there, stopping your thoughts from defaming your calm demeanor. Prayer does not necessarily have to be religious in nature. You can utter anything that makes you happy. For example, if you are an animal lover, the prayer can be about your pet. Keep yourself relaxed and breathe slowly. Keep your breathing in check to eliminate any interruption caused by your thoughts. Each time you breathe out, think of the prayer you chose. The final step is to become aware of your surroundings. While staying in the same position, calmly open your eyes, and sit for a while. Think about the process and how different you feel after it.

Mindfulness Meditation

The second kind is mindfulness meditation; a combination of meditation and mindfulness. It is a state in which you're fully aware of who you are, your thoughts, and your feelings. You let go of all the negativity around you and completely focus on yourself. There are different ways to practice mindfulness meditations but one of the simplest and most effective ways to do this requires a comfortable environment and a few minutes of your time.

The steps involved in this meditation are very similar to that of spiritual meditation. It involves finding a calm place to sit in where there are no distractions. Notice your breath carefully; the air that you are inhaling and exhaling, how your stomach is moving, and the time interval of every breath. It is okay to pause to make adjustments. Shift with intention at a time that is convenient for you, giving space between what you are experiencing and what you decide to do. While doing this, notice your thoughts. The main aim is not to suppress those thoughts but to acknowledge them. If you feel overwhelmed by those thoughts, focus back on your breathing until you feel better.

Movement Meditation

Another type of meditation is movement meditation. Most meditations encourage you to stay in one posture, but it may be difficult for some people to sit in one place and focus on their thoughts. Movement meditation emphasizes the mobility of the body. This type of meditation involves being mindful. You start noticing the body parts that you normally over-looked. You notice how your body moves and become more aware of your interior feelings. There are several ways to do this meditation.

Dancing is a fantastic entry point into movement meditation because it requires no skills or training to begin, and it's also a lot of fun! Put on your favorite music and start exercising your body freely when you're alone at home. You'll start with just one song, but as you practice, you'll be able to add more. You'll eventually want to make three or four music playlists for your move-and-mediate sessions. Be aware of each body part while you dance for your anchor. Begin with your feet and focus all of your attention on them. Then you'll slowly scan your entire body, noticing and letting go of all the sensations that arise.

To prepare yourself for movement, begin meditating while running as soon as you lace up your shoes. Reduce the rate of your breathing and focus on the work at hand. Use the sound of your feet thumping on the ground as your anchor once you've hit the pavement for your run. Allow distracting ideas to fade away as you take each stride. Bring your thoughts back to the beat of your stride when it wanders.

Walking is a great low-impact option if you prefer to move slowly. Choose an area where you can take your time walking. (A long hallway, as well as a backyard or a field, might suffice.) Bring your attention to your feet and feel your toes for the duration of each stride as you walk. Take 10 to 15 steps, then turn around and do it again. The sensation of your foot lifting and lowering is your anchor. To stay connected to your feet, walk with purpose.

This one comes with a bonus. You get a clean house in addition to a clear mind! Many cleaning tasks include repetitive motion, which is ideal for meditation. It allows you to concentrate on the movement's rhythm. Inhale as you extend your arm long and exhale as you bring it back in when vacuuming. Make sure you're not slouching by maintaining a good posture. Pull your navel to your spine and maintain a calm gaze. Allow the movement's rhythm to assist your body to relax.

This type of meditation does not require a place. Normal day-to-day activities can also be a form of meditation. The things that we do regularly like washing clothes or cooking are a part of movement meditation. It depends on what works well for an individual. Another kind of moving meditation is walking meditation. This can be practiced anywhere.

Focused Meditation

Focused meditation entails concentrating on something for a long period of time in order to stay in the present moment and slow down the inner dialogue. Unlike traditional meditation, where you quiet your mind by clearing your thoughts, focused meditation allows you to stay in the present while focusing entirely on one item.

Focused meditation has a number of incredible advantages. It can help you reduce stress. It can aid in anxiety management and the development of self-awareness. It makes you more creative and imaginative and improves your attention span.

For this meditation, you need to find a comfortable spot and a target for your focus. Fully relax your body and turn your attention to your chosen target. For example, if you're focusing on a painting in front of you, pay attention to the sound, smell, sight, and specifics of your concentration point. Attempt to let go of the stress that is running through your body. Breathe deeply from your belly button. You can cross your legs or not; the important thing is to keep your body as relaxed as possible while maintaining proper posture. The aim is to maintain a quiet mind. If your mind wanders and you begin to think about stressful situations, divert your focus to your chosen target. Even if you are unable to completely focus on your target, do not worry and stay calm.

Visualization Meditation

The next type of method is visualization meditation. It may seem a little contradictory to combine visualization with meditation because meditation is about clearing your thoughts. Visualization meditation is a method in which an image that evokes a specific mood or quality is brought to mind. We envision something that is not really there, which is a form of escape from the world. It is a technique for calming the mind while the body is relaxed by visualizing pleasant images, concepts, and symbols.

For this meditation, sit straight in a chair and breathe deeply through your nose. While concentrating on your breathing, visualize a specific outcome. If you want something, picture yourself with that thing as if you have already achieved it. It is important that those visuals are as vivid as possible because that's what makes them powerful.

If you're having trouble visualizing, take a step back and think of an old friend or a place you usually hang out at. When you think about something or someone you like, your mind naturally embraces the image, details, and all, without exerting too much effort. If your attention wanders to other thoughts, be patient with yourself and gently guide it back to your original focus, avoiding self-judgment.

Meditation offers numerous health benefits on its own, including lowering blood pressure, slowing heart rate, and calming the mind. Furthermore, visualization might assist you in making steady and consistent progress toward your goals. When both of these are combined, the benefits increase.

You'll develop a more positive mindset through this technique. You'll discover how to let go of negative self-talk that's been keeping you back for years. You'll be able to focus on your goals and handle the challenges that come your way. Meditation sessions are frequently associated with an increase in energy. You'll feel more physically energetic as your body relaxes. You'll feel more mentally energetic as well. Furthermore, as you continue to practice, your motivation will grow as well.

Chanting Meditation

The last type of meditation is chanting meditation. Chanting meditation is a type of meditation that uses sound to induce altered states of awareness. Sound has the ability to heal, calm, or stimulate. Chants of sacred words, mantras, and prayers are all used in meditations. It necessitates a state of tranquility as well as a desire to look within.

The first step involved is choosing a mantra. Some mantras can be as simple as vowel sounds while others are aimed toward a specific goal. These include deity mantras, healing mantras, and chakra mantras. Once you have a mantra in mind, the next step is to find a quiet place. Set a time so you know when to stop but make sure that the alarm tone isn't too loud. Take a few deep breaths and chant your mantra silently. Try to match your mantra with your breathing pattern and eventually it will set into a rhythm. Any unwanted thoughts should not be forced away. Feel whatever you're feeling and keep chanting your mantra. Even if the timer goes off, take a few minutes to sit with your quiet mind.

Through this meditation, we begin to understand how our mind works. It helps us get rid of the negative energy around us. We have a remarkable potential for carrying around things that aren't ours, such as rage, guilt, envy, and so on. Mantra meditation provides a secure entry point into a higher viewpoint of our own thinking. It calms our nervous system and fills our hearts with compassion for ourselves and for others.

Use of Senses

Beyond our five senses of taste, touch, smell, sight, and hearing, many of us have heard of a sixth sense. Our sixth sense, our intuition, is as much part of our body as the other five senses. However, it may take some time to get accustomed to it. You can use your five senses to develop intuition.

Do you ever get a weird feeling in your throat whenever you're waiting for your teacher to hand out your exam paper? Does your heart feel light after hearing good news? Our body works well with intuition. If a person feels like something is wrong, they feel a tingling sensation in their skin or may get goosebumps. Some people can get a stomach or a headache. In order to find out how your body processes intuition, pay attention to how you feel in a certain situation.

If you allow yourself to feel it, you'll be able to tell if your intuition is present. It will cause goosebumps on your skin, a shiver down your spine, a race in your heart, and a quickening of your breath. It can be even more subtle at times, and the only way to explain it is as a "knowing." When something is right, you'll know because it feels obvious, fulfilling, and enriching. And you'll know when something isn't quite right, for example, a dull pain or a flattening sensation. If you're not used to trusting your intuition, it may be challenging at first, but give it time and believe it gradually if that seems better. It will be well worth the effort.

If you are a visual person, you may be able to picture things using your third eye. Just like our two eyes, our mind has a third eye that gives us information. Whenever we close our eyes and picture things, we're using our clairvoyance. All you have to do to start trusting your intuition when it comes to seeing things through your third eye is close your eyes, quiet your mind, and envision a scene related to what you want to learn more about. Another way that intuition works with your sense of sight is by giving you signs that can be seen by your physical eyes. Did you ever want something badly and a billboard appeared in front of you? Our mind automatically starts seeing things that we want.

Intuition frequently manifests itself as a voice in your thoughts. It's termed "clairaudience" when you "hear" guidance like this. You must quiet your mind and listen to the thoughts that occur in order to develop intuition by listening to your inner guidance. We can also hear this guidance through the words of others or even music.

Let's say you're unsure about your college options. Your intuition will help you choose the best course of action. Make a mental note to pay heed to any advice you receive. If you're not paying attention, your intuition won't be able to communicate with you. When you begin to pay attention, good things will begin to happen. Just give it a shot and see what happens.

Smell and taste are primitive sensations that are closely linked to our survival instinct. While clairalience is associated with the fifth chakra in the throat, it is also linked to the root chakra. Clairalience, like any other intuitive sense, can provide particular knowledge about a significant other. You may smell their fragrance and feel connected to them. Likewise, you may enter into a library and the smell of old books makes you feel connected to the place.

Dreams

Have you ever awoken in the middle of the night with weird objects creeping into your mind? For instance, snakes, knives, or fire? The cognitive mind is at rest when you sleep, allowing your subconscious mind—your intuition—to convey its needs.

Dreaming is a natural source of intuition and asking a few simple dream questions can lead to major intuitive breakthroughs. They offer advice on healing, spirituality, and dealing with tough emotions. Intuition is frequently manifested in dreams. Sometimes, a dream can make zero sense, but at other times, they try to communicate with us. If you're an intuitive person, you will try to find the hidden meaning behind every dream.

In order to interpret the meaning behind every dream, you need to ask yourself how the dream made you feel and what kind of reality was presented to you in this dream. Your dreams may help you make decisions, link you with deceased loved ones and spirit guides, warn you of impending troubles, and inspire and motivate you. All you have to do now is pay attention.

Dreams can send us both positive and bad messages about ourselves, others, and life in general. In your sleep, you're subconsciously trying to activate your psychic abilities. No matter how much a person tries to remember a dream, it is sometimes impossible. Keeping a dream journal by your bedside can make it easier to remember dreams. Jot down all the important information; the place, the characters involved, the situation. Write down how you were feeling in your dream and after you woke up. Do this right after you wake up because the longer you wait, the harder it is to remember what the dream was about.

Before finding out what the metaphorical meaning of your dream could be, try to focus on the literal meaning. For example, a dream that you got into a fight with someone could be a result of being apart from that person for a long period of time. After interpreting the literal meaning, you can move on to the metaphorical meaning of what the dream symbolizes.

We all have unique experiences and perspectives that make our dreams personal. If you're having the same dream over and over again, creating a dream dictionary would be useful. Recurring symbols can also indicate to recurring events and feelings in your life, providing a way to confront and heal them.

The most essential thing to remember is to concentrate on how the dream made you feel. If you woke up in tears after a dream that was objectively happy, there was certainly something you missed.

The feeling we evoke in our dreams is often the most vivid memory we have of them, and this is the most important clue to deciphering their meaning. Use the feeling as a guiding theme for your interpretation and see if you can place the dream's events in the context of it.

Paying attention to our dreams might give us knowledge that we might not have access to while waking. Turn your mind to any unresolved difficulties or worries before you go to sleep. As you drift off to sleep, consider various options or resolutions. Close your eyes and leave the rest to your brain.

Cartomancy

Tarot cards are an excellent tool for developing intuition, especially cards with a lot of symbols, colors, and objects to provide further layers of intuitive interpretation. When using the cards, apply what you believe in to help improve your intuition and personalize it even more. The cards are best utilized as a tool for any views you hold, not as a belief system or a "rule-maker" system in and of itself.

After you pull out a card, take some time to evaluate it. Analyze the colors used, the symbols, and the patterns. Archetypal symbols are depicted on each card. These symbols are eternal in nature and allude to global topics. They have subliminal recognition. They elicit an emotional response as well. You can journal about what you think the card's advice is saying to you and how you plan to incorporate it into your day.

An individual's logical mind talks us out of believing in intuition. Tarot cards form a story that diverts our logical mind from reasoning and that is when our intuitive insights kick in. Intuition is intangible. Tarot cards provide you with something concrete to assist you in gaining access to something immaterial. This reduces the feeling of stumbling in the dark.

There are some steps involved to awaken your intuition by using tarot cards. The first step is to invite your spirit guides or those who care about you to join you in the session. You do not have to literally invite anyone. You can do this by meditation as well. After that, pick a card from the tarot deck with the intention of strengthening your intuition. Place your card upside down without looking at it or guessing what the card could be. The third step is to write down what comes to your mind. Turn your card over to find out if your thoughts have anything in common with what the card represents. Finally, trust yourself and your intuition.

Intuition is an intrinsic element of all of us, according to astrology; however, some signs have more intuition than others, and each sign has various intuitive skills. Each of the twelve astrological signs represents a different method in which intuition can work its magic. There are four zodiac signs that are the most intuitive.

Cancers are known to be highly intuitive. Cancers have a powerful emotional capacity. They can sense when something is wrong even if they don't know what to do about it. When you're down, being around a Cancer can help you feel the support you need, even if you don't mention what's wrong. Their main problem is that they do not trust their own intuition. They're usually always correct, yet they tend to adjust their methods or minimize themselves in front of the people they care about.

Scorpios are always aware of their surroundings. They have the ability to see things that others cannot. No matter how hard you try to hide the truth from a Scorpio, they will always find out. When the universe calls Scorpio with intuitive abilities, Scorpio must determine what to do with this energy sooner or later. It's not uncommon for the universe to send a persistent second and possibly third wave of intuitive energy to grab the attention of this sign that prefers life on its own terms. Self-mastery and achievement come from learning to transform bad tendencies into good expressions.

Aquarius is one of the most intelligent signs, which comes as no surprise. They're continually attempting to grasp what's beyond the reach of most other signs. While other intuitive signs have a more mystical approach to accessing intuitive knowledge, Aquarians have a more practical and proactive attitude to whatever they accomplish. As a rule, this sign thinks quickly and may be unaware that it is acting on an instinctive urge. A continual motivation is to find new and exciting life pursuits. Feelings are stored within a logical framework; thus, this isn't a very emotional sign. Aquarius' inventiveness is ingrained in its DNA. When a desire to defy established routines arises, intuition appears almost by accident. The brain of Aquarius is intrigued when the universe sends waves of insight toward this lighthearted personality. This sign is enticed to move forward in unusual ways by the challenge that intuition delivers in the shape of a puzzle.

A Pisces intuition is hardly ever wrong. They have a better understanding of life than any other zodiac signs. They have the ability to feel everything around them deeply. They're fast to adjust to new situations and perceive things from a variety of angles. Dreams and the arts are popular ways for the universe to enter Pisces' reality. Having faith in intuition is a test for Pisces. When Pisces' belief system and ambitions are combined, creative potential emerges. This sign is more focused and balanced as a result of sound reality testing. The promise of intuitive chances is diluted by denial and excessive escapism. Directly confronting hardship brings inner clarity and draws achievement. It can be helpful to recognize that an excessive desire to make things perfect can be the adversary of good and inner serenity.

Nature

When we're among other people, we tend to talk to them and act in a socially acceptable way. As a result, we pay less attention to nature and miss out on opportunities to interact with it.

How do you make a connection with nature? It's common knowledge that spending time in nature is beneficial to one's mental and emotional health. When you connect with the rhythm of the natural world, whether it's taking a stroll through a park or hiking by a tranquil stream, you're moving at the same pace as Earth and its elements. In reality, making physical contact with the earth can help you feel more grounded, generating a sense of balance, clarity, and, in many cases, intuition.

Spending time alone in nature and listening to what it has to offer is the greatest way. When you spend time alone in nature, you're more likely to notice what's going on around you.

Pay close attention to what's in front of you, ask questions about it, and enlist the help of nature for intuitive answers. Because nature puts you powerfully into the present now, being alone in nature will boost your intuitive talents and eliminate mental distractions that impede you from receiving guidance. Bring all of your senses to work and try to notice every detail of your surroundings by seeing, smelling, hearing, and feeling them. Concentrate your efforts on whatever catches your attention the most.

You can connect with nature while walking, which has its own set of advantages, but your body is more grounded, and your mind is at ease when you sit down. Take a seat, relax, and take in your surroundings.

Nature provides a relaxing and centering influence that can assist you in accessing your intuition. Take a walk outside and think of a problem that you're facing. Play close attention to nature and the objects around you. Ask your intuition what insights this object can give me about my problem. Explore new places, places that are normally out of your comfort zone. You may find the answer to your question. Just taking out three to four minutes a day for yourself and being separate from other people for a while can help you get in touch with your intuition.

You may have observed how relaxing you feel after a walk in the woods or while you're walking. Connecting with nature has a significant effect on us because it harmonizes our internal rhythms and makes us feel at ease.

It's no surprise that when we're around nature, our intuition abilities are enhanced. That's because connecting with Mother Earth elevates our energy, allowing us to effortlessly release fear-based energy, emotions, and mental chatter we've absorbed during the day. Our energies oscillate at the same frequency when we connect with nature, creating the same tranquility that Mother Earth has.

Follow these three methods when using nature to help you awaken and enhance your intuitive abilities, to increase your sensory awareness:

- To improve the neural network responsible for intuition, you must concentrate on your senses. The senses you should concentrate on include sight, smell, hearing, feeling, and tasting. The first stage in training your intuition in nature is to develop your sensory awareness.

- You practice gaining knowledge from the natural world to connect with nature and train your intuition with its support. In all elements of nature, there is profound wisdom to be gleaned. The elements, crystals, plants, oceans, and even organisms are all examples of this.
- When you're out in nature, sit in meditation and start a discussion with whatever element you've chosen.

Fear of stepping outside of our comfort zone is often the impediment to awakening our intuitive abilities. This dread of stepping outside of your comfort zone and into an unfamiliar area could be the reason you're unable to access your intuition.

Here are some ideas for breaking out of your comfort zone:

- To begin, determine that you are open to and committed to prioritizing the awakening of your intuitive abilities, even if it means stepping outside of your comfort zone.

- It will be much simpler to break free from your comfort zone after you have made this clear intention and commitment to yourself.
- Make time in your calendar to go out in nature and start cultivating your intuition.
- Keep a journal of your progress to see how far you've come. In a short period of time, each modest step you take will add up.

Although intuition is powerful and can lead to incredible insights, you should not follow it blindly. It's still crucial to utilize common sense and a healthy dose of logic. To position yourself to make the greatest judgments, you need a balance of both— bring both the intuitive and intellectual sides of your brain into play.

CHAPTER 11
EMPATHS AND INTUITION

ALTHOUGH IT IS COMMONLY BELIEVED and reported that empaths are intuitive individuals, and this is true for some, there is no requirement that an empath is intuitive or that an intuitive has a high level of empathy. While a few people believe the terms are interchangeable or that they are inextricably related, the truth is that not all empaths are intuitive, and not all intuitives are empaths.

In reality, the two attributes—empathy and intuition—are indeed very distinctive in one crucial aspect. When you study the terminology, you'll discover that empathy is the capability to perceive and experience the feelings and energy of various individuals and your environment in a broad sense. It is mostly about feeling outward emotions. Turning inward and accessing your subconscious mind and "gut instincts" to analyze and comprehend a scenario is what intuition is all about. It does rely on gathering and processing information from the outside world, but the final ingredient is mostly internal.

As a result, it's a mistake to assume that individuals who have a lot of empathy also have a lot of intuition. They are separate components of an individual's temperament that should not be lumped together into a unified attribute.

Where the two powers intertwine is where Intuitive Empaths are birthed. So why are these individuals known to hone both empathy and intuition?

Psychic aptitude that manifests as a feeling of knowing, receptivity to telepathy, tendency to get messages in dreams, the potential for fauna and flora contact, and ability to receive gut feelings and bodily cues are all characteristics of intuitive empaths. Intuitive empaths have a strong sense of intuition and sensitivity, which they can use to direct their life. Empathic psychics are able to read other people's feelings as if they've been acquainted with them for years. They are acutely aware of others' wants and desires, and have the ability to hear, see, and experience them. Emotional profundity enhances perceptions, and a powerful intuition is a characteristic of an empathic psychic.

There are several signs that can help distinguish intuitive empaths from other types of empaths. Here are a few examples:

1. They are well capable of distinguishing between their own and other people's emotions. The absorption of other individuals' emotions into one's own mind and body is a big challenge for many empaths. Their absorbed energy combines with their own, polluting their own consciousness. Since they can't discern what's theirs and what's not, they typically end up becoming like people that surround them. For example, they grow harsher when they meet angry people; when they see an anxious individual, they become so themselves, and when they see grief in others, they become melancholic. As for intuitive empaths, things are extremely distinct. They are so in touch with their internal state that they can readily distinguish it from whatever they may pick up from their environment. They are hardly affected by other people's feelings. Although

they may still perceive and experience these sentiments, the effect on their own state of mind is much less pronounced than for other empaths. They are excellent at establishing a porous yet manageable barrier separating their personal emotions and those of and others. They have the flexibility of allowing the two to blend; however, they can easily split them up for the majority of the time.

2. They are able to see through emotions and get to their root cause. Although empathy enables you to recognize and internalize others' emotions, it does not tell you why they would be going through them. This might very well be the basis of considerable perplexity for nonintuitive empaths as they begin feeling things they don't fully comprehend. Nevertheless, one of the characteristics of an intuitive person is the capacity to look at things from a bird's eye view, which enables them to see the connections present beneath the surface. Intuitive empaths see details that other empaths don't, and they use their subconscious to dwell on what they perceive, giving them an understanding of why

someone is behaving a certain way. These folk don't exactly do it on purpose; it's just a natural inclination and ability that arises from possessing a lot of empathy and intuition. An intuitive empath can occasionally have a deeper awareness of an individual's thoughts than the individual themselves.

3. They assist folks in comprehending their own emotions. An intuitive empath has most likely been helpful to a lot of people in the pursuit of understanding what they're experiencing and, essentially, why they're experiencing it. They generally love conversing with others regarding their feelings, ideas, dreams, and concerns. They are quite articulate with putting their thoughts into words. They can understand people's logic as well as put themselves in their position from an empathetic perspective. These aid in the construction of a fuller image and the identification of possible causes for their emotions.

4. They are the ones who most seek guidance and advice. Intuitive empaths make excellent consultants because of their ability to

comprehend and understand others' sentiments, as well as their proclivity for taking a broader view on things. When others are faced with an issue for which they cannot see remedy, Intuitive empaths are most likely the first people they turn to. Another thing that intuitive empaths are known for is inventiveness. Intuitive people are innovative, and their ability to think beyond the box makes them excellent problem solvers. They possess the ability to recommend alternative approaches to the problem and weigh the benefits and drawbacks of each.

So, are there ways in which you can sharpen your empathic intuition and in fact turn it into a super-power? You bet there are! And not just 1 or 2 or 3 but 20! Read this list to learn to better your empathic intuition and if you think you aren't an empath, go back to *Section 1: Empaths and Empathy* and learn how to begin one. You can then refer to these tips to also become intuitive.

1. Take some time to meditate.

Because intuition sends you silent signals, investing in silence will aid you in both discovering and analyzing them.

2. Begin to notice everything with traditional senses.

This can help you become more sensitive to the sixth sense.

3. Give heed to what you're dreaming about.

The brain does get overworked at times, and when that happens your intuitive parts of the brain might be overridden. While you sleep, however, your brain relaxes, allowing your unconscious to communicate with you through dreams.

4. Be inventive.

Painting, journaling, or writing are examples of artistic endeavors that calm the mind and enable your instinct to sharpen.

5. Use oracle cards as a guide.

Before consulting a handbook, learn to utilize a tarot deck to decipher the meanings without assistance.

6. Put your hunches to the test.

Should you have any suspicions about what may occur in the future, jot them down and check them afterward. See how many times you were correct.

7. Use your body as a guide.

Your intuition communicates with you via your body, and as you become more somatically aware, you also get more receptive. Give heed to if you acquire an uneasy physiological sensation while making a decision. It could be a light or heavy feeling, a sinking feeling in your stomach, a headache, or diarrhea. This might be your intuition speaking loudly and clearly to you.

8. Take a break from your regular schedule.

Since it's difficult to be alert to the gentle sounds of intuition when you're overworked, attempt to empty your calendar and observe if your intuition responds.

9. Go for a walk in the woods.

The natural environment can help us reclaim the type of instincts our ancestors honed.

10. Use what you've learned in the past to help you in the future.

Recall a bad encounter from your history, preferably one that happened recently. Consider whether you had any feelings that told you to stay away before this happened. Perhaps you had a gut sensation that things weren't quite right. Perhaps you experienced a dream or vision that foreshadowed what was to come. Recall as much information as you can. The more you can connect with the side of you that warned you, the more likely you are to believe it the next time.

11. Allow yourself to feel more and think less.

The mind is prone to overthinking. Intuition, in contrast, has a physical sensation. The key is to distinguish between thoughts and emotions.

12. Make a habit of moving in the same way.

Participate in repetitive activities like dancing, playing, instruments, or even cooking. These can help you listen to your intuition.

13. Be consistent with your principles.

Your head may lead you astray from your values, but your intuition will never do so. Your intuition would keep you from compromising your beliefs. You'll begin to notice your intuition more vividly in accordance with your principles.

14. Get in the habit of tapping into others before you get to know them on a personal level.

Before you converse with people, observe them and feel their energy profile to see what type of information you may gather.

15. Develop your intuitive abilities.

Intuition can be studied in both formal classroom settings and online programs.

16. Let go of your aversion.

When you have an instinctive hunch, don't dismiss it. Rather than trusting intuition, the conscious mind frequently debates it. Get into the habit of believing in your instincts.

17. Begin a new breathwork session.

Breathwork, or the deliberate manipulation of the breath, can quickly provide profound insights.

18. Make a conscious decision about who you associate with.

People that deplete you will cause noises that will make it harder to understand what your gut is trying to tell you. People who nourish and strengthen you should be kept, while those that empty you should be avoided.

19. Keep your eyes peeled for your environment.

Take as much input as you can receive from your surroundings; this will add more knowledge to your subconscious and subsequently make your intuition precisely guide your judgments.

20. Be willing to rid yourself of negative emotions.

Negative emotions hamper intuition, which is why making poor decisions is so easy when you're furious or sad.

PART FOUR
HIGHLY SENSITIVE PERSONS (HSPS)

CHAPTER 12
WHAT IS AN HSP?

ARGUMENTS, achievements, and even injuries affect all of us in various ways. But consider the interesting aspect related to what degree of impact do we all experience from experiences that are similar more or less. It might sound like a foreign concept to some but we all can experience and actually do experience different things while existing in the same environment and going through similar experiences. People who tend to experience intensified reactions to their surroundings are termed as an HSP (highly sensitive person). These are individuals who happen to possess a sensitive nervous system and are affected by subtle aspects of the environment. Now the interesting thing that one must note down is the fact that an HSP does not have a disorder or a disease. They in fact have a trait and there is absolutely nothing "quirky" about it.

Psychologists have declared HSPs to be a subset of a certain population who have an increased personality trait that is described as sensory processing activity or sensory processing sensitivity (SPS). These increased levels of SPS result in an individual displaying an increased emotional sensitivity along with a stronger reaction to external as well as internal stimuli that includes pain, light, sounds (mostly noise), and even hunger.

Highly sensitive people have a stronger "yes" or "no" response to emotional imagery, according to the MRI scanner, especially when it comes to those who are "near to them."

"What we notice with a particular assignment is that the brain of HSPs lights up in more locations beneath the MRI scanner than non-HSPs," Van Hoof explains. This is referred to as "deeper processing." As a result, HSPs think differently from non-HSPs. Their minds work in various ways. HSPs are frequently advised that they overcomplicate things and go too far with their interpretations. They frequently have a "weird" feeling about them.

As a result, the power that comes into contact with HSPs is substantially greater. As a result, you could argue that an HSP's brain is always attentive and ready to respond to others.

A person who is highly sensitive will likewise "pause and weigh" more frequently. This can also be detected in the area of the brain responsible for motivation, cognition, and emotion processing (amygdala). When HSPs strive to avoid things or show obsessive behavior when they are rejected in love, for example, this section plays a role.

HSPs will make additional decisions based on their schooling. In the eyes of another, a sensitive child will wish to do "good." But, then again, what is "good" depends on the child's or the setting's environment.

Positive and negative stimuli affect HSPs differently. They are influenced not just by their senses (hearing, smell, taste, touch, vision, and feeling), but also by rejection or acceptance signals. The amygdala is in charge of processing emotions, among other things. The HSP brain appears to be always on guard mode at times. HSPs are sensitive to prospective risks and are wary of committing mistakes since they dislike having their faults pointed out to them. Receiving congratulations or pointing out their strengths does not go down well. HSPs are constantly at odds with themselves. They will only see criticism as a negative, and a "no" can feel like a personal rejection to them.

The amygdala is ultimately responsible for determining if a stress response is required, such as when a (emotional) stimulus is too strong. This triggers a chain reaction in the adrenal glands, resulting in the creation of stress hormones (with endogenous excretion as a result). Learn to recognize the symptoms so that you can respond quickly if necessary. This causes blood pressure and heart rate to rise, as well as muscle tightening. The body prepares to fight or flee by sharpening its senses.

More and more people have started to self-identify as highly sensitive and this concept has gained traction in the last few years due to this. HSPs tend to feel much more disturbance from things which include violence, a sense of being overwhelmed, and even any kind of tension. The more positive side, however, is that these individuals also form a higher sense of appreciation of beauty. They would end up perhaps enjoying a sunset far more than an individual who does not have the same level of sensitivity. They feel happiness more intensely even display higher levels of gratitude and creativity as well. Their relationships also tend to be more meaningful and richer, and this is a reflection of the fact that HSPs actually end up also experiencing much more beauty in their lives than other individuals.

The more popular discussion that arises on this topic and that has managed to attract attention in the recent past is the question as to whether being an HSP is actually a disease or disorder. Consensus narrates that it is in fact a personality type and not a disease or disorder. Just like honesty, dishonesty, resilience, and other traits can exist in an individual to different degrees, so does being an HSP and can vary from person to person.

Most information that we come across identifies the fact that hypersensitivity makes you experience pain and emotions more intensely. But another significant aspect is the fact that it might also provide you with some adaptive advantages. It also has been shown to heighten brain activity in useful areas of your brain and there is also a tendency to be more optimistic, useful, and even indulge in social behavior. HSPs are also more self-aware and demonstrate much more empathy toward people around them. You would find an acquaintance or even a complete stranger showing more interest in your day's events or how you are feeling as compared to perhaps even family or friends. It is not that each one of these kinds would be an HSP, but often this trait dictates such ability to understand and empathize with people.

As far as the survival instinct is concerned, being an HSP might be a revolution as well as an evolution that ends up saving the entire mankind. SPS strategies that include empathy and calmness may allow deep integration along with social information, which even eventually might end up fostering survival as well as alliance and cooperation.

While speaking of HSPs, we cannot ignore the fact that it is perceived differently in different cultures and even science describes it differently for different genders. Most or almost all cultures consider men to be strong and emotionally in control of themselves. This kind of personality trait has managed to attract negative attention from people in some cultures where men who demonstrate such behavior are considered to be weak. Women are generally considered to be the "softer" gender and are often dealt with differently when it comes to such traits. Which also makes us wonder: Is being an HSP the same as being an introvert? The answer may not be that straightforward. Although 30% of the HSP population is considered to be extrovert, more often high sensitivity is seen to overlap with introversion. And the thing that must be noticed is the fact that even the population that is extroverted is perceived as shy by others.

There are so many questions that puzzle us often with this nature of personality and the next one is that are HSPs the same as empaths? Those who have been interested in studying empathy have managed to argue that the traits are definitely not mutually exclusive. Empaths tend to sympathize with others, read their moods, and even comprehend their feelings well. They also end up absorbing the moods of others. Also, HSPs possess these qualities too, they have not been declared as the same by psychologists yet.

Empaths and HSPs both tend to need time to be on their own, are sensitive to noise and light, have also shown an aversion to a large group of people. It is also observed that it takes much longer for them to unwind after a day that has been hectic and busy. The key point here is, however, that HSPs are usually introverts while empaths can either be introverts or even extroverts. HSPs are also seen to share the love of music, nature, and even a quiet environment with empaths. They also share traits such as the desire to help other people and live a meaningful life. One can be both HSP and an empath and in terms of an empathic spectrum, empaths will be found on the far end whereas HSPs will be found a little bit further in on the spectrum.

There are often those who then bring us to the next question of whether HSP is the same as autism? This is a rather important question and for the purpose of elaborating this topic, it cannot be ignored. Focuses on the two tend to find overlap and this is where the confusion arises. This overlap often ends up raising the point that these may be the same thing just with different names. This is because the diagnosis revolves around sensory experiences that are shown to be different than most of the population.

Both theory, as well as research, has revealed that SPS has been found in almost 20% of the human population. HSPs have been found to be associated with identifiable genes, multiple patterns of brain activation, behavior, and even physiological reactions. As discussed earlier, this trait has been found to be a major contribution to increasing survival skills by enhancing awareness of opportunities like food, alliances, and even possible mates, as well as threats.

Multiple studies have been conducted over the years that have tried to analyze the attentional aspect along with the perceptual one in humans where they were expected to observe any changes and differences in photographs of landscapes. These revealed that HSPs demonstrated a higher level of brain activity while observing certain aesthetic visuals as compared to other individuals.

Have you ever compulsively scrolled a social media page, or have you ever been overwhelmed during the days of intense lockdown? Those intense emotions are what the regular life of an HSP feels like. This is the simplest way to describe the overall existence of SPS and how it works. SPS is the scientific name for an HSP and is in fact a heritable trait and is usually measured on a validated scale, which is often used to evaluate the sensitivity level of kids and adults. HSPs have multiple traits and their trait of SPS is independent of other traits in their body.

A few volunteers were considered at UCSB Psychology Building where they were shown some happy and some sad faces while also given some context in each situation. Several interesting things were taken into account, especially the fact that while this entire process was taking place, the subjects demonstrated a deeper brain activity and processing, and this is a clear sign of a high level of sensitivity. Most people will also find themselves troubled and often find it hard to focus and this is why scientific experts have also recommended them to take a break and give themselves space to process and understand their emotions better. A lot of scientific articles have also highlighted the fact that it's often more helpful to indulge in activities and deal with emotions differently.

Review the following checklist to find out if you're an HSP!

Check all that apply

You are easily startled.

Regardless of whether you're extroverted or introverted, you find the desire to devote a lot of time to solitude.

You have a powerful unpleasant reaction if you come about violent things.

When you are confronted with beauty, you get a profound pleasurable response.

You're quite sensitive to noise.

Strong fragrances, even pleasant ones, overwhelm you more than others.

You used to be extremely particular about what you dressed like as a kid, making decisions based on how everything felt.

You're extremely attentive to time constraints and deadlines.

Your parents or school may have labeled you as "gentle" and "calm" as a child.

In "busy" areas like pubs, nightclubs, concerts, gatherings, and festivals, you become overloaded.

Your dreams and nightmares are vivid.

Whether it's via your human interactions, religious beliefs, or world philosophy, you're always looking for purpose.

You observe details that others overlook.

You feel transparent in comparison to others.

You have a tendency to tear easily.

In your romantic connections, you want substance.

You frequently ponder life's greater meaning.

You have a hard time transitioning.

When something is coming to an end, you may find it difficult to let go.

When you're famished, it's difficult for you to concentrate, and your temperament suffers as a result.

You might feel uncomfortable and jittery as a result of someone observing you perform something that you're actually good at.

You go to extraordinary lengths to organize your life in such a way that you are not overtired.

You appear to require more rest than others.

CHAPTER 13
STRENGTHS OF HSPS

BEING an HSP can be a powerful asset. All HSPs have their own special abilities, and these are only a handful of the many possible sensitive talents. If you're an HSP, you've probably heard the phrase "Why are you so sensitive?" a few times. And it might come across as a snide remark or even an insult. However, there are some significant benefits to being "very sensitive."

HSPs are more likely to become overstimulated and weary as a result of high amounts of information because they pay attention to details in their surroundings and are more emotionally affected by social stimulation. If you're an HSP, you may notice subtle changes in the environment that other people usually don't pay attention to. An HSP would notice any slight change in someone's appearance. If your friend is not well or if something is keeping them up at night, you would be able to tell if you're an HSP.

In many situations, this attention to detail is a beneficial attribute. You have a keen sense of others' likes, dislikes, and preferences, and this sensitivity can help you make friends and allies immediately. HSPs are good at holding conversations and making friends easily as compared to non-HSP's. They put the needs and comfort of other people above theirs, which makes it easier for them to interact with people.

Sensitive people are acutely aware of how their actions in the past can now affect the future. Sensitive people strive to build the finest possible future by reflecting on related events from the past and considering all possible possibilities of how their decisions may affect the future. This wish isn't just for their personal future; it's for the future of humanity as a whole.

HSPs have heightened insights and perceptions. The brain of an HSP is programmed in a way that helps enhance perception and self-awareness. They always think before acting. HSPs are constantly taking in a lot of information and thinking carefully about it.

They are defined not only by their empathy but also by their ability to understand the needs of others and their genuine concern for injustice. They take a very broad approach to their work perspective. This makes it easier for them to step outside of themselves and connect with the world around them. From an emotional standpoint, these people may be affected by the realities of others. They have a cognitive side as well, which is their worry, interest, and urge to reflect and understand the human being.

HSPs have a stronger emotional response to both positive and bad events in their life; their highs and lows are higher and lower, respectively. They feel too much, which could be both a good and a bad thing. For example, if an HSP passes a test, they might feel overwhelmed with joy, but if they fail a test, they might be extremely sad.

HSPs aren't only attuned to their own emotional world; they also quickly pick up on the feelings of others, and often end up feeling those sensations themselves. This means that if their friend finally gets a job after years of hard work, they would also be happy for them. Likewise, if someone is being treated unjustly in front of an HSP, they would feel bad for the victim.

HSPs have a deep perception of others' feelings, wants, insecurities, and so on. HSPs have more active mirror neurons, which are responsible for perceiving others' emotions, according to science. Their emotional intelligence and sensitivity make them a natural at communicating, resolving conflicts, and motivating people. Unfortunately, they may start people-pleasing and prioritizing the needs of others before their own. Their civility, kindness, and conscience are frequently appreciated. They are undoubtedly known for these attributes. While these characteristics are vital, sometimes they can get in the way of their success because people might start taking advantage.

HSPs use their emotions to intuitively connect with and understand the world. They are usually fantastic listeners since they take someone in suffering seriously and don't reject their feelings as unimportant or insignificant. While many people provide counsel on how to get over it as quickly as possible, they recognize the value in being there to listen without judgment or agenda. Do you know a person who is famous for being a great listener and whenever you face a problem, you go to that person to share? It is possible that the person is a sensitive person. However, this does not at all mean that other people are insensitive or not great listeners.

We are aware of other people's moods and intentions, and we may be able to sense their emotions to some level. Bianca Acevedo conducted a study in which sensitive and no sensitive participants viewed images of strangers and loved ones expressing happiness, grief, or neutral feelings. Sensitive people showed higher activation in the areas of the brain related to empathy in all scenarios where emotion was displayed, but especially when looking at the pleasant faces of loved ones. Sensitive persons showed increased activation in areas signaling that they wanted to do something after viewing images of their loved ones who were unhappy, even more than in areas related to empathy.

HSPs can successfully interpret and resolve interpersonal issues. They despise conflict and are sensitive to others' feelings and needs, allowing them to operate in peaceful surroundings. Only once HSPs recognize that they are highly sensitive can they use emotional intelligence to their advantage. This awareness allows them to gain from their increased emotional awareness while also recognizing and combating their bad tendencies.

HSPs are great at relationships. They might take some time to create bonds with people and open up completely, but once they do, they go all in. They mesh their energies with the person they're with which helps them in understanding the other person.

HSPs spend too much time and energy in maintaining meaningful relationships with people they are interested in. HSPs take a stand for what's right. All of their senses are heightened, causing them to live by emotion rather than reasoning. As a result, their approach is more "relationship centered" than "agenda based."

Love is a psychological strength as well. It's the ability to know how to devote oneself to others, to look after one's connections, and to comprehend the reasons for one's feelings. This isn't only about romantic relationships. If one of extremely sensitive people's strengths is love, it's because they know what they are doing when it comes to comprehending what this dimension entails. It entails showing concern, giving affection without being obnoxious, and respecting the privacy and needs of others. It's understanding that love is founded on reciprocity, on emotional rather than violent communication.

You might be an HSP if you've ever had a strong feeling of awe at art, music, or literature.

HSPs grasp the complexities of human language and emotion. They most likely have an artistic streak or a strong sense of inventiveness. They like to convey their emotions through vivid metaphors and figures of speech, aiming for words that truly capture the significance and beauty of the cosmos. The world is a strange and lovely place to them. HSPs have a broader perspective on the world. Many artists, authors, singers, and performers are sensitive and creative, giving them the ability to impact people via their work. This is because of their strong sense of imagination and attention to detail. They are extremely quick learners. An HSP can learn a language or a skill much more quickly than a non-HSP.

Their body's physical state and responses can be delicate, even if they have a sensitive disposition and intellect. It's possible that the bare minimum of medication is all they need. They may enjoy coffee, but one cup in the morning will provide them with enough energy to last for a couple of days as compared to friends who may require more.

HSPs are fascinated by fresh ideas, new techniques, and things that consumers did not even realize they required. They also appreciate reimagining and repurposing existing products or ideas.

Introversion is a trait that many HSPs have, and it's a trait that can help them be more creative. The emotionally sensitive have a high level of sensory sensitivity, making them sensitive to shades, concepts, colors, and textures in the commercial world that most people don't notice. They can also detect voids, gaps, and opportunities for creativity that others can't.

HSPs don't seek extravagant parties to attend or expensive plans to be part of. A simple conversation with a friend in a coffee shop is sufficient. They even find pleasure in the smallest things—grocery shopping in an almost empty supermarket, going for a run, and reading a book with a cup of their favorite drink. These little things are easily accessible for HSPs, and they culminate the ingredients of a happy, relaxing lifestyle.

People who are very sensitive have a better understanding of their role in the world. This may take a long time for them to do, with many disagreements and battles along the road, some of which they will win and others of which they will lose. The majority of them, on the other hand, gain a better grasp of who they are and how they can function in everyday life and in their interpersonal interactions. They are able to do so because of their valuable aptitude for introspection and contemplation. It means that they're always able to figure out why things happen the way they do.

One of the most common misunderstandings about sensitive people is that they are bad communicators. The opposite could not be further from the truth. The capacity to "read people" is one of the characteristics of great sensitivity. It's not just about picking up on other people's behaviors and reactions; it's also about picking up on their internal feelings, emotions, and intentions. As a result, sensitive people can customize their communication style, content, and delivery to their target audience.

CHAPTER 14
CHALLENGES FOR HSPS

DO you continuously feel physically and emotionally exhausted? There is a chance that you're an HSP. Being an HSP comes with its pros and cons.

If you're an HSP, you know how stressful life can be at times. When you're exhausted, you're exhausted. You're incredibly hungry if you haven't eaten in a few hours. When something awful happens to you, it might linger for days or weeks, and even when everyone else tells you to go on and get over it, you're constantly replaying the event in your head. The worst part is that you're afraid of seeming like you're complaining or exaggerating when you try to convey how you feel to others. As a result, you frequently find yourself saying nothing.

You're in the minority if you're an HSP. HSPs make up about 15–20% of the population, which could indicate that you grew up with folks who were not sensitive and didn't understand your sensitivity. It can be challenging to have your experiences acknowledged, and it might make you wonder why you do certain things in your life. You may have even wondered what was wrong with yourself at times in your life. That's why it's helpful to learn about the issues that other HSPs face on a daily basis.

Being overly sensitive, on the other hand, is not a weakness. It's just another way of expressing what it's like to be human. The highly sensitive feature is a typical biological difference in which all of the senses are heightened and perceived more intensely, according to research. This characteristic has also been discovered in over 100 other species. This attribute indicates that you are easily overwhelmed, but it also indicates that you possess some special abilities that most people lack.

Do you have a habit of overanalyzing conversations, people's facial expressions, and so on? Your excessive sensitivity has a lot to do with your overthinking. HSPs are typically aware of clues in conversations that others are unaware of. During a conversation, for example, you may be more aware of someone's body language, facial expression, tone, and voice porosity.

It can be difficult for an HSP to go through the world especially if they haven't yet realized that they are, in fact, highly sensitive. They can be confused as to why it appears that others have it easier than they do. Or they might frequently think as to why they seem to be more emotional than most people. Perhaps they are exhausted or overwhelmed by things that have no effect on others. This universe is not designed for delicate individuals. In fact, our world is well built for individuals who are disengaged. This is a difficulty for persons who are extremely sensitive.

The whole discussion on empathy earlier was true. The life of an HSP is subconsciously influenced by the emotions of the people around them. If their sister woke up in a bad mood, the HSP can be prone to starting their own day off on the wrong foot, too.

Being a very sensitive person might provide a number of difficulties. HSPs may find it difficult to adjust to new conditions, exhibit seemingly inappropriate emotional responses in social contexts, and get easily irritated by light, music, or specific physical sensations.

For HSPs, being mentally and emotionally drained can be a very common problem. An HSP tends to absorb the emotions of other people. If you're an HSP and you're in the company of a depressed or anxious individual, you are going to absorb all their emotions and exert all your energy. It is difficult for such a person to not feel something.

Extremely sensitive people may also find it difficult to establish limits. Even if they are deeply concerned about the needs of others, they are prone to over-looking their own needs. They have a hard time saying "no" or asserting themselves because they prioritize the needs of others. HSPs have a proclivity for picking up on other people's wants and senti-ments. They despise disappointing others. This can be taxing and has a long-term effect. HSPs frequently absorb or take on the emotions of others, and it can be difficult for them to discriminate between their own feelings and those of others.

Going to a bar, throwing a party, or hanging out with a large number of people is what many people do for enjoyment. HSPs prefer quiet time and being in a crowded or noisy environment for too long can over-whelm them. Not only that, but physical stimuli can also exhaust HSPs. To some, small things like a hazy

TV or fluctuating lights may not seem like much, but they can easily overwhelm HSPs. If this describes you, you're probably aware that while you may be able to identify what is upsetting you, you may not always be able to articulate why it is hurting you. HSPs digest all stimuli more thoroughly than nonsensitive people, so what others consider insignificant and unimportant might appear large and overpowering to HSPs.

HSPs also tend to be perfectionists. They avoid making mistakes that could lead to exhaustion and burnout. It is important for such people to maintain their reputation and work on pleasing people in an unhealthy manner. HSPs have a stronger reaction to criticism than non-HSPs. As a result, they may go to great lengths to avoid being reprimanded, such as working overtime, which can lead to burnout.

HSPs are sensitive and gentle individuals that demand a different approach than others. Conflict and criticism, which are considered commonplace in everyday life, can, however, irritate HSPs. Non-HSPs may find this to be one of the most difficult facts to grasp and alter.

Understanding HSPs, on the other hand, involves comprehending that yelling at them, scolding them, or being irritated with them can cause them to shut down. This type of interaction might be extremely painful for the HSP. And the HSP who is constantly injured will stop communicating or interacting altogether for fear of receiving the same treatment.

HSPs love alone time and normally want to spend that time sleeping. However, it may be difficult for them to fall asleep or sleep without disruption. This is a regular occurrence among HSPs. They're sensitive to various kinds of stimulation, including noise, temperature, textures, and the degree of activity in their surroundings, and this can make it difficult for them to fall asleep. Even when they are in severe need of rest, they may find it difficult to relax and drift into dreamland.

HSPs may discover that they have too many thoughts to fall asleep, in addition to their bodies being wound up. They process our experiences profoundly, so they may be wide awake until their minds have had time to wind down, even if they ask their brains to "shut down" for the day. They may require more sleep than others due to their depth of processing. They miss out on a vital opportunity to recover and reset their overworked senses when they don't get enough sleep. Running on little sleep can feel like hell for the HSP, since every tiny irritation and inconvenience is amplified by a factor of ten.

Another challenge for HSPs could be pessimism. HSPs are more prone to rumination and self-doubt since they are their own worst critics. If they make an unpleasant mistake, they may remember it for a long time and be more mortified than the ordinary person. Have you ever done something really embarrassing in front of your classmates? We all have. An HSP would be haunted by this kind of occurrence forever.

It is also difficult for them to work under pressure. When they are attempting something difficult, they don't like being observed and evaluated, and the stress of being observed can induce them to make mistakes. They are more likely to be perfectionists, but they may also be more conscious of how stress is not unavoidable and how it affects them. They can express their entire creativity and intellect because there is less pressure and time limits. Working under duress, on the other hand, is extremely stressful for HSPs and causes them to perform poorly.

Change is difficult for anyone, but it is especially difficult for HSPs who thrive on routine. As a result, even positive changes, such as a pay raise or promotion, can cause people anxiety. This may be unusual for their friends and family, who are perplexed as to why they aren't experiencing the happiness of their sudden fortune or success. Even favorable changes can take a long time for HSPs to adjust to.

Low self-esteem, lack of confidence, and thoughts of not being good enough affect certain HSPs. This is most common if their sensitivity has been criticized or judged from an early age—if they were raised as a very sensitive child—making them feel humiliated or ashamed. As a result, many people try to please others and/or "fix" or rescue them, which is often an unconscious impulse to satisfy their own unmet needs.

No matter how great HSPs are at relationships, they also face problems. Many HSPs have had troubled romantic relationships in the past because their partners didn't appreciate their high sensitivity or need for space when they were overwhelmed. This has frequently resulted in a lot of friction and animosity on both sides. Many HSPs appear to strive to close off their feelings and wear a "mask" to hide who they really are in their early interactions for fear of being labeled as "too sensitive." As a result, their spouses are frequently unable (or unaware) of their genuine emotional requirements. That mask can place them in codependent relationships with needy partners, addicts, or narcissists—settings in which they don't sense a meaningful connection.

HSPs are extremely sensitive to pain and can be susceptible to "energy" or autoimmune disorders, such as chronic fatigue, fibromyalgia, or insomnia, while others struggle with allergies, intolerances, irritable bowel syndrome, and digestive issues. On a medical level, this could be related to food and chemical sensitivities, but on an emotional level, it could indicate a problem with HSPs "digesting" and processing other people's difficulties.

HSPs have a strong sense of compassion for others, which makes it difficult for them to say no to others. HSPs also have stronger mirror neuron activation, which leads to a higher sense of empathy, according to the study. Because they are more emotionally sensitive than the majority of individuals, they have a natural desire to please others. This great amount of empathy, though, can backfire. HSPs typically say "yes" even when they want to say "no" because they desire to satisfy people. They don't want to hurt or disappoint others. However, because they are unable to say no, HSPs frequently have too much on their plates and overlook the downtime that they require to function well.

An HSP who does not get enough downtime is a difficult person to be around. They become irritable, agitated, and irritable with others. Because HSPs tend to carry a lot of stress in their bodies, not getting enough sleep can lead to physical sickness.

PART FIVE
HOW TO STOP ABSORBING NEGATIVE ENERGY AND THRIVE IN TODAY'S WORLD— GUIDED MEDITATION

CHAPTER 15
GUIDED MEDITATION BASICS

A STATE of calm concentration is induced via guided meditation. Another person is normally in charge. They could be a yoga instructor, a religious leader, an audio book, or even a self-recorded CD. The guide directs you to relax specific muscles in your body until they are at ease, then guides you to visualize pictures and images. A healing light or the scattering of previous mistakes are common examples. It could be a few moments or several hours long. The goal is to relieve physical, emotional, mental, and tension in any scenario.

Guided meditation has been utilized as a medical care for decades. In the 13th century, Tibetan monks started to meditate while envisioning Buddha treating their illness. Others claim that this style of meditation has been around for a long time, possibly stretching back to the ancient Greeks and Romans. Nowadays, guided meditation is a generally recognized supplementary and alternative medicine technique, with clinics, hospitals, and medical professionals using it in conjunction with traditional treatments across the globe.

Various different religions and cultures have produced a variety of conventional meditation practices. Meditation is considered to have originated in 1500 BCE in the historic Hindu religion of Vedantism. Meditation was originally referenced in Western Jewish texts. These teachings were specifically centered around prayer meditation.

Imagery in Healing was published by Jeanne Achterberg in 1985. She accomplished so as an activist for holistic medicine and a trailblazer in guided meditation. This famous book investigates how visualization is used in meditation and the beneficial effects it has on disorders. It also examines how guided meditation can assist sufferers in coping with physical discomfort. This book blended current science with the practices of ancient healers, making it a landmark in the field of alternative medicine.

Marin General Hospital's Humanities Program was developed by Leslie Davenport in the late 1980s. Davenport was an influential proponent of guided visualization in meditation. *Healing and Transformation by Self-Directed Imagination*, a book by Davenport, concerns tantric yoga, a practice that inspired Buddhism and Hinduism and inspired adherents who think gods communicate with humans through imagery.

Benefits

Stress alleviation and a calmer, more receptive attitude toward life are two major benefits of meditation. According to Dr. Jon Kabat-Zinn, a molecular biologist, professor, and researcher at the University of Massachusetts Medical School, meditation switches brain activity from the busy, stress-housing right-frontal cortex toward the more tranquil left-frontal cortex. The elements of your brain that make you desire to be chaotic will be calmed by meditation.

15 HEALTH BENEFITS OF MEDITATION SUPPORTED BY SCIENCE

1. Stress reduction: Meditation has been found to help people cope with stress.

Stress-related diseases such as irritable bowel syndrome, posttraumatic stress disorder, and fibromyalgia may benefit from it.

According to neuroscience research, mindfulness practices diminish amygdala activity and improve interactions between the amygdala and the prefrontal cortex. Both of these parts of the brain help us to be less vulnerable to stress and to cope with stress more quickly. Meditation also could also help with anxiety.

Protracted meditation can assist in minimizing the likelihood of depression and alleviate preexisting symptoms, probably due to its positive effect on brain activity. The emission of mood-altering cytokines, an inflamed molecule that can support the development of depression over time, has been demonstrated to be reduced by a variety of meditation techniques.

2. Enhanced sleep: Meditation will assist you in falling asleep more quickly and getting a healthier night's sleep. Mindfulness and meditation can help you achieve a tranquil state of mind that will help you sleep better. This response is known as the relaxation response, which is the polar opposite to the stress response.

Insomnia is commonly regarded as a hyper-arousal condition, despite the fact that falling asleep includes a progressive decrease in arousal. Our brains remain "wired" when we are weary, depressed, or anxious, making sleeping more challenging. In the long term, we perpetuate this stress by connecting bedtime with anxieties of not being able to fall asleep.

Meditation generates a condition of acceptance and mindfulness, which lowers psychological suffering and enhances depressive moods and emotion regulation. Mindfulness, according to these researchers, could improve sleep quality by providing patients with the mental skills they need to prepare their nerve systems for sleep.

3. Controlling pain: Meditation can assist you in managing your emotions and reducing pain. This, in combination with medical care, can help with chronic pain management. Physical discomfort is not completely alleviated by meditation. As per brain scans performed in conjunction with a guided meditation study, it reduced brain function in areas connected with sensation, showing that it changes our relation with the experience. To put it differently, it will aid in the re-framing of pain in the brain, making it more manageable.

4. Decreased Inflammation: Inflammation is the body's way of responding to something it doesn't like on the inside. This can be a good thing in some cases since it implies that the body is combating an illness. Chronic inflammation, on the contrary, causes structural alterations in the body that were related to cancer, diabetes, IBS, and even Alzheimer's disease. Meditation, on the other hand, may be able to help mitigate some of the negative consequences.

According to Dr. Roizen, a study on the link between meditation and inflammation found that individuals who meditated had a significantly lower inflammatory reaction than others who didn't. This suggests that meditation may have the power to reduce chronic inflammation in the body.

5. Improved cardiovascular health: According to research, both mindfulness and Transcendental Meditation can enhance cardiovascular health and reduce the risk of heart disease. Meditation activates our bodies' "rest-and-digest" processes, which counteracts our "fight-or-flight" instincts. Integrating yoga into one's daily routine has been linked to decreased heart rate and blood pressure, potentially lowering the risk of heart disease.

6. Ability to concentrate better: Meditation improves concentration, which is important because so many meditation practices emphasize focus. In actuality, meditation has been demonstrated to aid in the fight against habituation, which is the propensity to resist devoting attention to new information in our environment. Mindfulness meditation has also been demonstrated to improve problem-solving abilities and reduce mind wandering. Furthermore, research demonstrates that mindfulness training can boost focus for up to 5 years, indicating that guided meditation can truly help you adopt better attributes.

7. Greater compassion: Performing meditation for people has been found to boost our capability to undertake action to relieve suffering in multiple well-designed studies. It does so by lowering pain-related amygdala activation while simultaneously boosting brain networks associated with good emotions and affection. The "default network," the part of our brains that ruminates on thoughts, emotions, and perceptions when we're not doing something else, quiets down in long-term meditators, meaning less contemplation about ourselves and our place in the world.

8. Enhanced interpersonal interactions: Meditation has been demonstrated to help people engage with others. It heightens your capacity to comprehend signs that suggest how others are experiencing and boosts your empathy. Meditation also increases emotional stability, reducing your vulnerability to bad influences in your life. Enhanced parent–child connections have also been linked to mindfulness. Mindfulness practice has been found in research to help parents of preschoolers and children with disabilities cope with stress, despair, and anxiety. Mindful parenthood has also been linked to more favorable attitudes in children.

9. Improved aging processes: Meditation may also help you remain young. Unmanaged stress is well recognized as one of the primary causes of premature aging. It not only harms the mind but also raises the risk of heart disease and possibly cancer. When blood samples from the end of research on the subject were compared to blood obtained before the general population, it indicated alterations in biomarkers associated with aging in meditators.

10. Fighting against harmful cravings: Binge eating is commonly referred to as mindless eating, and it occurs when there is nothing else to do. A study of overweight and obese adults found that by meditating for 10 minutes every day for 28 days, they were able to reduce craving-related snacking by 40% at the end of the trial.

11. Increased creativity: Several studies have shown that adopting meditation into your daily practice might help you improve your cognitive abilities. It will be much easier for you to come up with fresh ideas and be inspired as a result of this. Many well-known artists, writers, singers, and dancers meditate on a regular basis.

12. Enhanced memory: The cortex is in charge of mental functions such as learning, attention, and remembering. Regular meditation improves memory via increasing blood flow to the brain, which strengthens the cerebral cortex's blood vessel network. Meditating for 20 minutes every day, according to one study published in a reputable cognition journal, increases memory and concentration.

13. Managing addictions: One of the many beautiful benefits of meditation is that it can help people overcome serious addictions. Several different styles of meditation appear to have similar effects as Vipassana meditation. This medication has been proved to be particularly effective in helping people break their addictions to alcohol and opioids.

14. Improved immune system: Several studies have shown that meditating on a daily basis can help prevent a variety of immunological-related disorders. This is especially true when it comes to common colds, allergies, and infections. People with compromised immune systems are more susceptible to minor infections than others. For some persons, meditation is very effective.

15. Enlightenment: This is the advantage that this book is mainly concerned with. There's a rationale why most psychics, tarot readers, astrologers, and others practice meditation (particularly guided meditation). Meditation with a guide can assist increase oxygen to the brain. Research on practitioners has indicated that when they engage in problem-solving tasks, their brain scans show that more areas of the brain light up. This suggests that meditators can use a larger portion of their brain than the normal person. This is what additional sensory perception is all about. Being able to use more of your brain allows you to become more aware of what is going on around you. As a result, your psychic powers will be nurtured and will become much more distinct and accurate.

Enlightenment is a phrase that is frequently used to denote a greater level of understanding. Psychic abilities are exactly what they sound like. It's no wonder, then, that guided meditation is a big deal in the mystical realm. The guided meditation techniques and examples in this section will assist you in achieving all of the aforementioned advantages. In essence, this section is a manual that not only gives you information on how to improve your life but also resources to help you do it.

CHAPTER 16
TECHNIQUES

THERE IS no one-size-fits-all approach to guided meditation. In reality, there are various distinct ways to go about doing it. These several techniques are available for you to select and choose from, depending on your needs and desires. Here are a few different forms of meditations:

Transcendental meditation: This requires sitting silently for 15–20 minutes per day with your eyes closed, reciting a mantra. It's one of the most popular meditation techniques.

It's a strategy for bringing more serenity and quiet into daily life, as well as recognizing the importance of being present. This form of meditation can be good if you are looking for a higher purpose in life. Saying mantras that are in sync with one's aims can assist increase one's psychic powers.

How do I go about doing it? Don't be concerned! We've got your back. Here's a step-by-step tutorial on how to practice Transcendental Meditation.

1. Sit in a comfortable position with your feet on the ground and your hands on your lap. Avoid crossing your legs or arms.
2. Close your eyes and take a few deep breaths to relax your body.
3. Now open your eyes for a brief minute before slowly closing them again. The rest of the meditation will require you to close your eyes.
4. Recite a mantra in your brain. This could be a Sanskrit mantra you learned from a professional tutor or something you found relaxing on your own. Continue to repeat the phrase and refrain from thinking about anything else.
5. After 20 minutes, carefully reintroduce yourself to the outside world by moving around and stretching your body. You can stay sitting until you're ready to resume your normal routine.

Mindfulness Meditation: This is a cognitive training approach that aids in the relaxation of the mind and body by slowing down excessive or disorganized thoughts and releasing negativity. It mixes awareness and meditation. Mindfulness is a mental state in which you are entirely focused on "the present" and can recognize and acknowledge your thoughts, feelings, and sensations without being judged.

How do I go about doing it?

1. Locate a seat that provides a secure, sturdy sitting without roosting or hanging back. It could be a park bench, a chair, or a meditation cushion.
2. Take up a good vantage point. Sit up straight in your chair or choose any of the yoga postures. Make yourself at ease, but not too loose. Maintain a parallel relationship between your upper arms and your upper body. Maintain a downward glance.
3. While relaxing your body, slowly focus your attention to your breath.
4. Try to keep track of your breath. Feel your breath exiting and entering your nose physically. Make sure you take a breath in and a breath out between each inhalation and exhalation.

5. There are no restrictions on what you can think about here. You can let your mind wander for 5 minutes or so as long as you bring it back to your breathing.
6. Try to control your reflex actions. You have complete control over how you move your body. Even involuntary actions, such as acute itching or the impulse to cough, should be paused.
7. Remain in this state for a bit before deciding how you want to spend the remainder of your day.
8. When you're ready, open your eyes and raise your gaze to finish your meditation.

Meditation of love-kindness: This is a popular type of self-care that can benefit health and decrease stress. Many people who practice loving-kindness meditation on a daily basis will see improvements in their ability to forgive, engage with others, and accept themselves, among other things.

During loving-kindness meditation, you direct benign and compassionate energy toward yourself and others.

How do I go about it?

1. Cast aside some private time, even if it's only a few minutes, and relax. Close your eyes and relax your muscles while taking a few deep breaths.

2. Imagine yourself in a state of complete bodily, social, and mental well-being, as well as inner peace. Imagine feeling unconditional love for yourself, appreciating yourself for who you are and accepting that you are perfect in your current state. As you concentrate on this sense of inner serenity, imagine breathing out worry and breathing in sentiments of love.

3. Repeat three or four positive and encouraging sentences to yourself. "I will be joyful," "I will be complete," and "I will not give up" are examples of such lines. You can come up with phrases that reassure you personally.

4. After that, relax and experience sensations of comfort and self-compassion for a few minutes. If your mind drifts, softly take it back to these thoughts of love and kindness. Let yourself to be carried away by these feelings.

5. You have the option of maintaining this focus throughout your meditation or moving your

focus to loved ones in your life. Begin with someone who means a lot to you. Feel the love and admiration you have for them. Make a mental note of the sensation. If required, repeat the soothing remarks.

6. After you've preserved your sentiments for that person, bring other important individuals in your life into your consciousness one by one, and image them in perfect health and inner happiness. Then broaden your network to include more coworkers, family members, neighbors, and acquaintances. You can also choose to integrate people from different parts of the globe.

7. When you think your meditation is finished, open your eyes. Keep in mind that you will be able to go back in time and revisit the wonderful feelings you experienced that day. Internalize how loving kindness meditation makes you feel, then shift your focus and take a few deep breaths to bring those feelings back.

Spiritual meditation: It is practiced by people of various religions and civilizations all over the world. Some individuals use it to relax and relieve tension, while others use it to cleanse their minds and awaken and develop their relationship with something greater than themselves.

Spiritual meditation strives to improve one's understanding of spiritual/religious significance as well as one's relationship with a higher power.

How do I go about it?

1. Close your eyes lightly and lay your right hand over the center of your heart and your left hand just below your belly button.
2. Start paying attention to and communicating with your breathing. Listen to how it makes you feel. Feel how your body changes with each breath. Breathe comfortably.
3. Visualize a light within yourself. Take into account its qualities like tone and brightness. Get an idea of how hot or cold it is. Believe that this light will guide you to greater power.
4. Start tracking the light as it leaves your body and ascends toward the sky once you've become familiar with it. Keep an eye on it as it passes through the clouds and into the heavens.

5. Allow oneself to feel at ease and connected with the heavens. Take a peek around and get to know your surroundings. Spend as much time as you wish there, keeping an open mind to whatever happens.
6. When you're ready, bring your light back into your body. To return oneself back to the present, slowly twist and turn your hands and feet. To end the session, open your eyes.

Progressive muscle relaxation meditation: Edmund Jacobson, an American physician, established progressive muscle relaxation as a strategy for treating anxiety in the 1930s. In this technique, many of the body's major muscle groups are tensed and released alternatively.

How do I go about it?

1. Find a quiet, distraction-free location. Lay down on the floor or recline on a chair, removing any tight clothing and glasses or contacts. Place your hands on the chair's sides or on your lap. Take a couple deep breaths slowly and steadily. If you haven't already, take a few minutes to practice diaphragmatic breathing.

EMPATH & PSYCHIC ABILITIES: 165

2. Concentrate your attention on the places below while remaining calm across the rest of your body.

3. Forehead: Squeeze the muscles in your forehead for 15 seconds before releasing them. Feel the muscles tense and tighten. After then, steadily relax the tension in your forehead while counting for 30 seconds. Take note of how different your muscles feel as you relax. Continue to relax your forehead until it is completely stress-free. Inhale and exhale slowly and evenly.

4. Jaw: Maintain a 15-second clenching of the jaw muscles. Then, while counting for 30 seconds, progressively let go of the stress. Continue to breathe slowly and evenly while observing how relaxed you feel.

5. Neck and shoulders: To generate neck and shoulder strain, raise your shoulders up to your ears and hold for 15 seconds. Slowly release the stress as you count for 30 seconds. Keep an eye on how the tension is diminishing.

6. Arms and hands: Make fists with both hands slowly. For 15 seconds, pull your hands into your chest and squeeze as hard as you can. After that, slowly release go for 30 seconds

while counting. Take note of how at ease you are.

7. Buttocks: Gradually increase the stress in your buttocks for 15 seconds. Then steadily release the stress over the period of 30 seconds. Keep an eye on how the tension is diminishing. Continue to breathe deeply and evenly.

8. Legs: Gradually increase the stress in your quadriceps and calves for 15 seconds. Squeeze the muscles as hard as you can. Then steadily release the stress over the period of 30 seconds. Take note of the tension decreasing and the lingering feeling of relaxation.

9. Feet: Gradually increase the tension in your feet and toes. Tighten the muscles to their utmost potential. Then, while slowly releasing the stress, count for 30 seconds. Keep an eye on how the stress evaporates. Continue to breathe gently and evenly in and out.

10. Continue to unwind for as long as your heart desires. Slowly stretch out your body and open your eyes when you're ready to leave the session.

There are several other meditation techniques, but listing and explaining them all is beyond the scope of this book. These, on the other hand, are the most important/useful, particularly if your goal is to improve your psychic talents.

Let's look at the many postures in which you can sit to get the best outcomes now that we've looked at meditation techniques. You'll find a detailed list below that will help you learn and comprehend the purpose and skill of each contemplative position.

Full Lotus position: The Lotus position is arguably the most well-known yoga pose today, even among non-yogis. It is often regarded as the "classic" yoga stance. Lotus is a common meditation pose that is used to begin or end many yoga classes.

The Lotus position is supposed to assist the practitioner prepare for profound meditation by relaxing the mind. Stretching the elbows, ankles, and hips also strengthens the spine and upper back. This position also promotes circulation in the spine and pelvis, which may aid in the relief of monthly discomfort and depression in the female reproductive organs.

1. Sit on the floor with your legs extended, spine straight, and arms at your sides.

2. Bend your right knee and hug it to your chest. Raise your right ankle to the crease of your left hip, with the heel of your right foot toward the sky. The top of your foot should rest on your thigh's crease.
3. After that, bend your left knee. The top of your right shin should be crossed over the top of your left ankle. Your left foot's sole should face upward, and the top of your foot and ankle should rest on your hip crease.
4. As much as possible, bring your knees together. Keep your back straight and your groin pressed against the concrete. While resting your hands on your knees, your palms should be facing up.
5. Make a circle with each index and thumb while holding the rest of the fingers in the Gyan Mudra position (index finger and thumb form an "O" shape, other fingers stay straight, face palm upward).
6. Soften your expression by bringing your gaze to your "third eye," the space between your brows. Hold for up to a minute, or for the duration of your meditation session.

Half Lotus Position: It's a seated posture that opens the hips and stretches the knees and ankles. It's a modified form of the Lotus Pose, a popular seated meditation pose, designed for persons with limited lower-body flexibility.

The Half Lotus helps to strengthen the back. Also stretched are the hips, elbows, ankles, and thighs. Sitting upright with the spine balanced calms the mind, reducing tension, anxiety, and moderate depression. This pose also improves pelvic circulation and blood flow, which can aid with menstruation pain.

1. Sit on the floor with your legs extended, spine straight, and arms at your sides.
2. Bend your right knee and hug it to your chest. Raise your right ankle to the crease of your left hip, with the heel of your right foot toward the sky. The top of your foot should rest on your thigh's crease.
3. When bending your left knee, cross your left ankle under your right knees.
4. Place your hands on your thighs, with your palms facing up or down. Keep your spine straight.
5. Close your eyes and turn your head inward. Hold for up to 1 minute, or for the duration of your meditation or pranayama session.

6. Release the pose by stretching both legs along the floor and sitting up straight. Hold the stance for the same amount of time with the opposing leg on top. Release the pose by lying on your back with your arms away from your sides and your legs apart and rest for at least 5 minutes.

Burmese position: This position requires the practitioner to sit on a mat with a cushion if needed, bend their legs with the right foot on the outside, and gently draw their feet into the pelvis. Their toes should be in contact with the mat.

1. Lean forward slightly and take a seat at the front third of the cushion.
2. Simply relax the muscles after straightening your spine by envisioning the top of your head pressing upward to the ceiling and extending your body in that direction.
3. With your buttocks up on the cushion and your stomach pulling forward a little, there may be a tiny bend in the lower area of your back.
4. Keep your spot. Holding the body upright in this position requires relatively little effort.

Seiza position: Some people prefer kneeling to sitting when they meditate. Buddhists in Japan invented this posture, known as the Seiza pose. You place a cloth, cushion, or soft material between your thighs and calves. Next, take a kneeling position. Check your physical posture before you start meditating to make sure your back is straight and your muscles are relaxed.

1. Kneel down in a comfortable position.
2. Your legs should be folded underneath you, and your feet should be turned up.
3. Your buttocks should be supported by your upturned feet.
4. Place your hands on your lap.
5. Maintain the posture.

Chair position: The chair posture may be a suitable fit for you if you're having problems with any of the other poses. It is entirely acceptable to sit in this position; it has no effect on the meditation. In fact, even sitting in a chair while meditating has multiple advantages. One of these advantages is the ability to properly ground yourself. Because the majority of your body is not in contact with the ground, your feet are the only point of contact. This meditative practice revolves around your feet. They represent how hectic your life is, but your feet keep you anchored.

1. Take a seat in a chair.
2. To assist grounding your body in this pose, keep your feet flat on the floor.
3. Place a cushion underneath you on the chair and sit on the forward third of it, much like you would on the floor, if that helps.
4. Sit forward in the chair to support your spine; if you must lean into the back of the chair because of back difficulties, place a pillow between the small of your back and the back of the chair to keep your spine straight and upright.
5. All of the factors of posture that are crucial when seated on the floor or in Seiza are equally vital when seated in a chair.

CHAPTER 17
SCIENTIFIC BACKING OF MEDITATION

MEDITATION AND MOOD Boosting

Researchers at Johns Hopkins University analyzed 47 trials (including over 3,500 people) and determined that mindfulness meditation programs could help with anxiety, according to a meta-analysis published in *JAMA Internal Medicine*.

In a 2012 study of 36 trials, meditation groups outperformed control groups in terms of anxiety symptoms. This was confirmed by 25 out of 36 people. Around 70% of the subjects reported improvements in their symptoms. In the realm of psychology, that is a statistically significant finding.

A modest NCIH study (in which 54 adults participated) looked at the results of a type of mindfulness-based stress reduction (MSBR) tailored to deal with insomnia (mindfulness-based therapy for insomnia, or MBTI) and a self-monitoring program. Both meditation-based programs improved sleep, but MBTI significantly lessened the degree of insomnia when compared to MBSR. Statistically significant results have repeatedly demonstrated how meditation can help with anxiety and that guided meditation is especially useful for sleep problems.

According to study, meditation thickens sections of the brain, including those connected with attention and introspection—and a "larger brain" equates to more control. A study found that meditating for 40 minutes a day for 2 months was adequate to increase brain volume in areas associated with stress, learning, memory, empathy, perspective, and compassion, implying that cognitive function could be improved.

In a 2011 NCCIH-funded study of 279 persons who engaged in an 8-week Mindfulness-Based Stress Reduction program, changes in spirituality were connected to improved mental health and quality of life.

Meditation and Pain Management

Meditation's ability to treat pain has been studied extensively and has consistently yielded beneficial results. Meditation, according to multiple studies,

EMPATH & PSYCHIC ABILITIES: 175

stimulates certain areas of the brain in reaction to pain. As a result, the discomfort becomes more bearable and less of a nuisance.

According to a relatively small 2016 study funded in part by the National Center for Complementary and Integrative Health, mindfulness meditation does help to reduce pain without the use of the brain's natural opioids. This suggests that combining mindfulness with painkillers and other pain-relieving treatments that rely on opioid action in the brain could be particularly effective.

According to a study published in the *Journal of Neuroscience*, meditation can help you manage pain. Fifteen people with no prior meditation experience were asked to just concentrate on their breathing in an MRI scanner; researchers alternated delivering a little amount of heat to their calves during the scan and asked them to rate their pain afterward to establish a baseline. The participants were given 4 days of mindfulness training before repeating the experiment. After investigating mediation techniques, they found a 57% reduction in unpleasantness and a 40% drop in pain severity.

In another NCCIH-funded trial from 2016, adults with persistent lower-back pain aged 20 to 70 received either mindfulness-based stress reduction

(MBSR) education, cognitive-behavioral therapy (CBT), or standard treatment. Even after the training was done, participants in the MBSR and CBT programs improved at a comparable rate, which was higher than those who received standard treatment. Participants in the MBSR and CBT groups improved their functional limits and back pain more than those in the standard treatment group at 26 and 52 weeks, according to the study. The results of MBSR and CBT did not differ significantly.

Meditation and Immunity

The American College of Gastroenterology revealed in a 2014 publication that the few trials that examined mindfulness meditation preparation for irritable bowel syndrome (IBS) had mixed, however, favoring positive results. The scientists emphasized that because the number of trials was small, they couldn't say if IBS was helped or not, although they did observe a positive trend.

In a study published in the journal *Brain, Behavior, and Immunity*, researchers taught participants mindfulness meditation or enrolled them in a general health improvement program. Since testing your skin is easier than testing your brain, they used a fiery capsaicin ointment to trigger an inflammatory reaction on their skin after 8 weeks. They discovered that those who meditated had a significantly lower inflammatory response than those who did not, showing that meditation can help the body mitigate chronic inflammation.

Mindfulness meditation, according to the findings of a 2011 NCCIH-funded study involving 75 patients, reduces the intensity of IBS symptoms after 8 weeks.

According to a 2013 study, mindfulness meditation helped IBS patients control their pain and improve their quality of life.

Meditation can help you stay healthy and avoid contracting a cold. In a research published in the *Annals of Family Medicine*, 150 individuals aged 50 and older were randomly assigned to one of three sessions for 8 weeks: mindfulness meditation training, moderate-intensity exercise training, or a control group. When compared to the control group, both meditation and exercise reduced their exposure to colds; during the trial, the latter two groups took slightly over half as many sick days as the control group.

Meditation reduces molecular markers of inflammation and has the ability to help manage the immune system, according to a 2014 assessment of science.

Eight weeks of mindfulness training can lower stress-induced inflammation more efficiently than a wellness program that includes physical exercise, diet education, and music therapy, according to the findings of a 2013 NCCIH-funded study of 49 adults.

Meditation and Cardiovascular Health

Transcendental Meditation (TM) can lower blood pressure in persons who are at risk of developing high blood pressure, according to the results of a 2009 NCCIH-funded study including 298 university students. According to the findings, meditation can help with mental distress, anxiety, depression, frustration/hostility, and coping abilities.

According to a literature analysis and scientific statement published by the American Heart Association, research supports the use of TM to decrease blood pressure. According to the study, it's unclear if TM is genuinely superior to other meditation practices in terms of lowering blood pressure due to the fact that there are little head-to-head trials. In any event, meditation lowers blood pressure, regardless of the type you chose to practice.

According to neurophysiological and neuroanatomical research, meditation may have long-term impacts on the brain, meaning biological data for favorable effects on the physiological baseline state and cardio-vascular risk. The physiological response to stress, smoking cessation, blood pressure reduction, insulin resistance and metabolic syndrome, endothelial function, inducible myocardial ischemia, and primary and secondary cardiovascular disease prevention have all been investigated in relation to meditation's impact on cardiovascular risk. Meditation appears to lessen cardiovascular risk in general, according to the study.

Meditation and Addiction

The findings of 13 trials using mindfulness-based techniques for quitting smoking had favorable results in terms of craving, smoking decline, and relapse prevention, according to a 2015 research study. Another study from 2013 found that meditation-based therapy can aid in the cessation of smoking.

Participants who underwent mindfulness training had a greater rate of tobacco use decrease both immediately after treatment and at the 17-week follow-up in a 2011 study comparing mindfulness training to a traditional behavioral smoking cessation therapy.

A 2013 brain imaging study found that mindful focus reduced the desire to smoke as well as activity in a craving-related brain area.

According to a study published in the *Journal of Behavioral Medicine*, a group of researchers developed an app that incorporates parts of meditation and mindfulness to help with cravings. For 28 days, a group of obese and overweight people meditated for 10 minutes each day. By the end of the research, they had reduced craving-related snacking by 40%.

Meditation and Cancer

According to guidelines published in 2013 by the American College of Chest Physicians, meditation can assist persons with lung cancer reduce stress, anxiety, pain, and despair while also increasing mood and self-esteem.

Meditation is prescribed as a supportive treatment for patients with breast cancer who are feeling stress, worry, sadness, or exhaustion, according to clinical practice recommendations issued by the Society for Integrative Oncology (SIC) in 2014. The SIC also recommends that it can be used to improve the quality of life for these individuals.

Meditation and Ulcerative Colitis

Anyone can have ulcerative colitis, however it is more frequent in those between the ages of 15 and 25. It's a very severe and unpleasant illness, with symptoms including weakness, joint inflammation, anemia, and weight loss, as well as discomfort, bleeding, and urgent diarrhea. It can have a detrimental impact on work and relationships, as well as an emotional and physical toll.

While there is no medical treatment for ulcerative colitis, research has shown that meditation can help with the condition. The following is a study that produced exceptionally encouraging findings in relation to the subject at hand.

In a 2014 pilot study, 55 people with ulcerative colitis in remission were divided into two groups. For 8 weeks, one group studied and practiced mindfulness-based stress reduction (MBSR), while the other was given a placebo. In terms of its advantages, the results were becoming progressively encouraging. Six and 12 months later, the researchers concluded that MBSR could assist persons in remission from mild to moderately serious disease—and possibly reduce stress-related flare-ups.

CHAPTER 18
GUIDED MEDITATION AND THE PSYCHE

SPIRITUALITY IS a wide concept that can be interpreted in a variety of ways. It comprises a sense of belonging to something bigger than ourselves, as well as a quest for meaning in life. As a result, it is a universal human experience that touches us all. A spiritual experience might be described as sacred, sublime, or simply as a deep sense of energy and interconnectedness.

Many people who include spiritual practice in their daily routines are yearning for something more. A recurring theme in this novel is higher purpose. Whether it's tarot, astrology, psychic powers, or meditation with healing crystals, the purpose of these practices is the same. It means being able to spiritually awaken and transcending one's usual human limitations. Whether it's for enhanced sensory perception or out-of-body experiences, meditation can help.

The topic at hand, spiritual awakening or getting in touch with one's psychic skills, becomes all the more simple when it comes to meditation. Below, you'll find techniques to practice guided meditation while working on and harnessing your psychic abilities.

Meditating with Crystals

Let's start with how you can use the power of crystals to meditate more effectively. Crystals can help you strengthen your extrasensory perception and get a deeper awareness of your own and others' psyches because they are a doorway into healing and spirituality, and some crystals have incredible psychic properties too (see Section 7 of this book for a more detailed discussion of crystal healing).

Crystals can help you improve your meditation skills. Chakra cleaning and relaxation can be achieved with colored crystals, while concentration and clarity can be achieved with clear quartz. Clear quartz can be held in either the expressive right or receptive left hand to radiate or absorb its strong energy. It can be applied to any part of your aura. Tuning to the resonance frequency of a faraway crystal and meditating on it may also be therapeutic.

You can meditate on the crystal or put it in your meditation bag to help you concentrate. Crystals can be used to cleanse and open chakras by placing the appropriate color crystal on the chakra of the same color and breathing through the chakra. Choose crystals that appeal to you from your favorite crystal shop. Putting together a useful set of tiny crystal pebbles should not be too expensive.

STEP 1: CHOOSING THE RIGHT CRYSTALS

Crystals might be chosen intuitively or based on patterns that others have noticed. You can easily buy one that appeals to you in a store and hold it in your hands while clearing your mind and observing how it makes you feel.

Clear Quartz

- Inexpensive
- Easily accessible
- The most beneficial for psychic clarity
- It establishes a link between us and our heavenly higher self

Amethyst

- This is a very mystical stone

- Easily accessible
- Aids in the development of insight into one's mind, self, and the path to nirvana

Selenite

- Exquisite quality
- Heightened vibrations
- Assists with internal peace
- Receives a lot of psychic information

Black Tourmaline

- Protective
- Soothing
- Absorbs negativity
- It helps you to stay grounded

Lepidolite

- Stress and anxiety management
- Aids in maintaining a peaceful state of mind
- Controls irrational thinking

STEP 2: PLACEMENT

Create a crystal grid by writing your intentions on a piece of paper (in this case, Psychic Nurturing) and placing it on the ground in front of where you will concentrate. Begin arranging your crystals on the paper in whatever pattern you think is most appropriate. You can also buy ready-made designs, but it's important to trust your instincts.

Crystal Mala necklace: If putting the crystals in a mala and wearing it around your neck feels more intimate (or convenient), go ahead and do it. If you're searching for a more intimate experience, this is the place to be. Since the stones are always in contact with your body, they absorb your energy and they could even pick up psychic information from the outside world and pass it on to you.

Holding in hands: If you don't have any other options or don't have the time to make a grid or bead a mala, you can simply hold the crystals in your hands. They will share all of the same advantages as mentioned above.

You're done once you've placed the crystals where they're supposed to belong. All you have to do now is meditate as usual and watch how the crystals can help you improve your meditation!

MEDITATING WITH TAROT CARDS

You can obtain a more deep and profound understanding of Tarot cards by meditating with them. It can also be a powerful self-healing tool, a strategy for manifesting, or a way to connect with the Divine. When we meditate with each Tarot card, we explore deeper into its meaning and symbolism. By bypassing the conscious mind, it allows us to communicate with our instincts.

By slowing our mind and letting go of the incessant mental chatter, we open the door to our subconscious mind and begin to tap into a higher level of wisdom and understanding. In this chamber, we let our intuition guide us, and as a result, we obtain a greater knowledge of the cards.

Step 1: Choose a card

Choose a Tarot card at random or one with which you want to interact more deeply if you're utilizing the Tarot card meditation to genuinely understand more about the Tarot card meanings. You can also choose a Tarot card based on a topic that interests you right now. If you were on a spiritual path, which is what this form of meditation is mostly for, the Hermit or a similar card would be a good choice.

Step 2: Set up an environment

Choose a time and place where you won't be disturbed for at least 20 minutes. Make sure you're comfortable, your phone is turned off, and the room is free of extraneous distractions. You can either sit quietly or listen to guided meditation audios. You may dim the lights and use essential oils to aid in setting the environment. Sit up straight and place your Tarot card in front of you.

Step 3: Breathe

Deeply inhale through your nose, focusing on the sensation of your breath on your nostrils. Deeply inhale, then gently exhale through your nose, focusing once more on the pressure in your nostrils. Continue to breathe while focusing on how the breath feels.

Step 4: Focus on the Tarot card

Keep your focus on the Tarot card in front of you. While softly gazing at the Tarot card, take five deep breaths. Simply watch any thoughts that arise in your head and visualize them flying away like clouds. Bring your attention back to the Tarot card in front of you, as well as to your breathing. Consider scaling up the card until the figures and visuals are almost life-size.

Consider entering the card in your mind. Take note of the finer points in your environment.

Look around again, imagining yourself as a part of the card. All you have to do now is keep your imagination alive and keep glancing around following each visual growth. It's time to progressively untangle yourself from the visualization and go back into the ordinary once you think you've seen enough and garnered some spiritual value.

Improvement in Psychic Abilities

Adolescents are the most likely to develop psychic powers. These abilities are passed down through family members (who either directly or indirectly teach us this language) or acquired in response to environmental variables. Because we are imbued with basic survival instincts that enable us to traverse the world securely, we notice more, see more, hear more, and feel more as youngsters. As we grow older, however, we are instructed to tone down our sensitivity, that spirits do not exist, and that pain is solely physical. As a result of this programming, we learn to believe that feelings and instincts are incompatible with science and reason, and we ignore our skills, criticize "clairvoyants," and accept the physical world as the sum total of reality.

But don't worry, your psychic abilities haven't been compromised. There are a variety of things one might undertake to reclaim one's psychic skills. The idea is to treat your psychic abilities as if they were a different creature, like a childhood buddy. To develop a new friendship, you'll have to get to know each other all over again.

It may sound cliché, but one of the most effective methods to access your psychic powers is to tap into your subconscious. We constantly set limitations in our daily lives to reduce the amount of stimulation we take in—and with good cause. In order to live good, functional lives, we literally cannot digest anything we come across. As a result, these perceptions are instead processed in our psyche.

Start meditating on a daily basis if you want to tap into your psychic powers quickly. The ability to tune into the spirit is at the heart of psychic abilities. It's critical to develop the ability to strike your core without exerting excessive effort. This will strengthen your psychic interaction with the rest of the world. Starting with a focused point to focus your mind on, such as a candle, is a simple approach to let go of your mind's mental wanderings. Simply take a few deep breaths naturally and without straining.

During your meditation time, you will begin to connect with spirit and your guides, which will aid you in developing true psychic abilities. Psychic meditation varies from ordinary meditation in that it is used to achieve a specific goal. Holding a crystal in your palm, such as white Magnesite or a combination of crystals, may help you achieve this goal. If you practice a certain psychic meditation every day, you'll soon be able to communicate with your guides, which is the first step toward enhancing these talents. Connecting with your spirit guide is a useful technique that is usually included in the development of these abilities. They may attempt to communicate with you in various ways, however, regardless of how they want to communicate with you. They want you to be aware of their presence. It's only a matter of being aware of their presence and acknowledging it. Recognize their presence and express gratitude for their support when they contact you. Relax and allow anything they want to show you to manifest in the most positive way possible for your personal growth.

But the question is, what psychic powers will you gain as a result of going to such extremes? Regular psychic meditation can help you develop a range of psychic talents or skills, some of which are more well-known than others. Since your outcomes and path may differ significantly from that of another individual, it's critical to know which of your senses is the most prevalent.

Let's look at the chakras that are in charge of communication. Your main sources will be the chakras that run from the throat up, and each chakra has its own set of crystals that assist you in working more effectively with the gifts that are regulated by that chakra's vibration. Keep in mind that purple amethyst crystals are a potent assistance in the development of psychic abilities and in the support of all of the higher chakras.

Throat chakra: The throat chakra stones exist in a range of colors, but when we think of crystals to treat this chakra, we normally think of blue healing stones. Some examples are blue sodalite, lapis lazuli, and blue kyanite.

Third eye chakra: You can use a number of powerful crystals and stones to energize and unlock this field. Purple scapolite and indigo kyanite are two examples of these stones.

Soul star chakra: Many stones with a high vibration are useful for awakening this chakra. Indigo kyanite, white datolite, and white selenite have all been found to be very helpful in this regard.

Adding stones that are appropriate for that aspect will speed up the process and help you attain excellent outcomes. There are numerous stones that can aid in the development of psychic powers. Many of the crystals listed below will help you improve your overall communication skills.

- Iolite
- Purple amethyst
- Labradorite
- Blue apatite
- Aqua quartz
- Azulite
- Blue topaz
- Rainbow moonstone

As previously said, each of these is better suited to a specific element, so choose the ones that best suit your needs.

The most important thing, though, is to include meditation into your daily life. You'll be well on your way to fine-tuning your abilities once this becomes the norm for you. During your daily meditation, it's extremely likely that you'll make contact with spirits, guides, and even angels, and that this will result in actual psychic abilities.

Heightened Sense of Self and Others

Meditation is the practice of contemplation or introspection in order to achieve a higher level of spiritual awareness or mindfulness. It is essentially a technique for calming the mind in order to achieve a different state of consciousness than the regular busy woken state. You learn to explore your inner dimensions through meditation in order to better understand yourself and feel the core of consciousness within.

Meditation is frequently used to calm the mind and body in order to alleviate a variety of health problems, including high blood pressure, depression, and anxiety. There are many different types of meditation, but in general, meditation is a practice that helps you to go beyond your active mind and into a state of serenity and tranquility. Your mind is clear, relaxed, and internally focused during meditation.

You are completely awake and attentive when you meditate, but your mind is not focused on the outside world or the activities that are taking place around you. Instead, your attention is drawn within. Meditation allows you to really focus on understanding your inner self because of the stillness and silence.

Here are a few ways to meditate to increase your psychic talents and self-awareness:

Qigong: Many people assume qigong to be a form of exercise, and they frequently confuse it with other Chinese exercises like tai-chi. Qigong, on the other hand, is a style of meditation that combines deep breathing and meditation with a series of steady, synchronized movements. Individual movements vary by tradition and instructor, but the overall purpose is to promote relaxation and self-healing through a combination of internal and external movement.

Many people believe that qigong can aid with pain management and the avoidance of a number of chronic conditions, with advantages ranging from enhanced flexibility and strength regulation to decreased stress. Due to the dynamic character of the practice, consider qigong as a technique to raise energy consciousness.

Vipassana: Vipassana meditation expands on mindfulness meditation by delving further into self-awareness. Vipassana, also known as insight meditation, is a type of meditation characterized by a curious and inquisitive consciousness. Self-observation as a means of self-transformation. Vipassana is a gradual approach to insight that can take years, unlike other methods that are largely event-based and can be acquired with practice.

It can open significant perspectives on yourself and your life experiences when practiced on a daily basis, generating a greater sense of calm overall. It's normally taught as a course, and it's often done as a multiday retreat. As a result, we consider vipassana meditation to be a technique for improving self-awareness.

Mindfulness meditation (Mentioned earlier in detail): Mindfulness is one of the most popular meditation practices in our community these days, thanks to apps like Headspace and Calm. On the other hand, mindfulness meditation is not a new concept. It is based on the ancient Indian practice of Samatha, in which the practitioner trains the mind to focus on a single object or characteristic in order to increase present-moment consciousness.

Many mindfulness practices allow you to focus on your breath, examining how air enters and exits your lungs, while gently observing your thoughts, emotions, and sensations. Thoughts can come and go without being judged, and when the mind wanders, the person just refocuses on the breath.

This exercise can be a fantastic source of relaxation and can help with anxiety management when one's own thoughts and feelings are placed into context. For our purposes, mindfulness meditation improves present-moment awareness.

Transcendental Meditation (mentioned in detail earlier): Transcendental meditation was the first meditation technique to reach the West. Maharishi Mahesh Yogi popularized it in the 1960s, and celebrities such as the Beatles and the Beach Boys endorsed it. It is based on a different ancient Indian custom.

TM focuses on the peaceful state of Being under the commotion of our ideas, as opposed to mindfulness meditation, which focuses on noticing thoughts. To "transcend" the domain of thought into Being, participants sit silently, breathing normally, and repeat a mantra, which is usually only a single phrase. TM has been connected to a number of benefits, including less stress, enhanced inventiveness, and quieter thoughts, to mention a few. Although mindfulness helps with present-moment awareness, TM helps with self-awareness.

Awareness of Others

Meditation has long been known to promote self-awareness. It also raises awareness of the people around us. In essence, it makes us more aware of what is going on and more present in our surroundings. Being aware of oneself and what is beyond is an important aspect of mystical conceptualism. Extrasensory perception as well is founded on the idea of being aware of more than meets the eye. Meditation allows us to focus our minds and ponder about things that are bigger than ourselves. It broadens our horizons and gives us a bird's eye view of life's happenings.

You might be wondering how meditation makes this feasible. So, here's how it's done. We are in a calm environment, entirely alone, and open to new thoughts and ideas while we meditate. During various meditations, our minds imitate the tabula rasa we are given when we are born. This indicates that we are a blank slate waiting to be filled. We think clearly about things that have to do with other people and our surroundings when we think about them. Meditation has been shown to reduce prejudices, which means we don't have any prior assumptions about the people we're talking to. This will help us rethink our relationships and give us a new perspective on people.

Considering psychics deal with people on a regular basis, this sort of meditation is extremely effective for them as their readings may be influenced if they have preconceptions or previous assumptions about the people who come to them. In reality, most psychics use guided meditation to keep their minds clear of preconceptions and biases.

Meditation, on the other hand, has been scientifically proven to enhance blood flow to the brain, which can cause it to thicken. When compared to nonmeditators, meditators use more of their brains. This means they have greater resources to carry out a variety of cognitive tasks. Such is the situation when we interact with other people. Our interactions are really a collection of cognitive functions, and the better our cognitive health, the better we will be able to deal with interpersonal connections.

FORMING NEW ABILITIES

Empathy

Because being compassionate usually includes putting others' needs ahead of your own, encouraging yourself to be nice requires not only diligence but also a little willpower. That's not to say that using religious or philosophical principles to motivate kindness will never succeed. It will take place. Any strategy that relies on constant self-control and top-down supervision of one's moral code, on the other hand, is guaranteed to fail. Perhaps more foolproof would be to cultivate compassion on a situational basis, such that it develops spontaneously when people are in need.

There's no need to travel far; the key to growing empathy is right in front of us. In mindfulness meditation, guided contemplation is used to help the mind focus. It usually entails sitting in a quiet location for 20 minutes to an hour (depending on progress) and learning to direct consciousness to the present moment rather than focusing on what has gone before or what is still to come, as previously discussed. The power of this practice to strengthen the brain and heal the body has recently been promoted, but for many of its most experienced teachers, the fundamental purpose of the practice is to help people heal their soul.

Researchers from Northwestern University recruited 39 persons in the Boston region who had never meditated before and split them into two groups. The first group finished an 8-week Buddhist meditation course led by a lama. The second group was placed on the course's waiting list. Participants were required to return to their lab one by one after eight weeks to complete attention and memory tests. The real experiment was conducted in a waiting area with three seats, two of which were already occupied by actors.

A third actor entered on crutches, wearing a boot designed for a fractured foot and wincing in pain a few minutes after the other participants and claimed the last seat. When she first walked in, she leaned against a wall, openly moaning because there was nowhere for her to sit. The other actors chose to ignore her on purpose. They were completely indifferent to her anguish as they thumbed through books or checked their phones.

In their study, the bystander effect was significant among those who did not meditate. Only 16% of the participants granted the crutch-wielding actor their seat. However, half of those who meditated offered their seat to the woman on the spur of the moment. The only difference between the two groups was that one practiced meditation while the other did not.

This study alone demonstrates that meditation improves empathy. After just 8 weeks of meditation, the number of people ready to assist the hobbling actress had tripled.

Sixth Sense

The sixth sense serves as a guide for you, supporting you in determining what is good and wrong. The sixth sense combines all of your other senses to create a tremendous force for you. While everyone is born with a sixth sense, many of us have no idea how to use it. Having a strong sixth sense assists you to make better choices. It's your sixth sense that helps you recognize positive and bad emotions before making a decision or taking a major step forward.

Meditation is the most straightforward way to get into your sixth sense. Meditation helps you relax your mind, which is vital if you want your sixth sense to work with you. As you meditate, your mind gets quieter and more relaxed. This allows you to hear your inner voice more easily. You should meditate for at least 10 minutes, if not more, every day.

Jagrat, svapna, shushupti, and turiya are the four states of consciousness according to Hindu beliefs. Jagrat is waking consciousness, svapna is dream consciousness, shushupti is profound sleep consciousness, and turiya is higher consciousness, which is above all preceding phases. The state of turiya necessitates inner silence. It is possible when the mind is free of mental barriers and attachments to time and location. Yoga and meditation are meant to help you achieve turiya, which is a sense of oneness with the universe.

If you meditate for a long period, you will develop "Siddhi" or the ability to see, hear, touch, smell, or taste things that are beyond your regular range of perception. These siddhis are a source of distraction, according to yogic common sense as articulated in Hindu texts. The real deal is about aligning with universal experience, which serves as a common basis from which all living and nonliving entities see reality. The Creator creates and protects this universe in the same way as the ocean perceives the moon, the earth and plant roots perceive the rain, minerals detect their atoms, and numerous birds, animals, and creatures see objects.

PART SIX
HOW TO STOP ABSORBING NEGATIVE ENERGY AND THRIVE IN TODAY'S WORLD— GROUNDING

CHAPTER 19
WHAT IS GROUNDING

AS AN EMPATH, especially one with psychic abilities, you would need to remain grounded at all times. But what is grounding? And why is it so important? The phrase "being grounded" has existed for a long time. It generally refers to returning to the earth, becoming focused, and reuniting with what matters most in life.

In essence, it is the direct contact of the flesh on our hands or bare feet with the earth's surface. It can also be done with the help of a grounding system. The beautiful thing about grounding is that for thousands of years, people from all walks of life have discussed the benefits of being barefoot on the earth and how it can enhance their health and well-being.

Grounding oneself is the process of balancing and linking your physical, emotional, mental, and energy states. We may feel lightheaded, fatigued, detached, bewildered, confused, disturbed, flighty, emotionally unstable, and so on if we are not grounded.

Is there science involved? Yep!

Grounding has been scientifically demonstrated to be therapeutic and restorative, lowering blood pressure, promoting sleep, and increasing blood viscosity, as well as reducing inflammation, tension, and discomfort. Connecting with the natural world may be the most beneficial treatment for your health and happiness. The medication is the earth's electrons, and it's all free. The difficulty is that we don't tap into this energy on a daily basis like our forefathers did in the past. They roamed barefoot and rested on the ground, or donned leather hides on their feet, and were constantly connected to the earth's organic vitality.

Every single one of us is a bioelectrical entity. To operate at our best, we have to be replenished like a battery. Think of the globe as a giant battery that generates a slight electrical charge in the electromagnetic field spectrum. We can recharge by attaching to the ground's electric nutrients, known as electrons, which provide a negative charge to the earth's surface. To function as nature planned and to limit the development of free radicals, our bodies require electrons.

According to one systematic review, grounding has an effect on the living matrix, which is the core connective tissue between living cells.

Electrical conductivity, like antioxidants, resides inside the matrix and serves as an immune system defense. They believe that by grounding, the body's inherent defenses can be restored. This idea will be expanded upon in future studies.

CHAPTER 20
BENEFITS OF GROUNDING

SO WHY SHOULD we bother with grounding? Well, the answer is simple. It has multitudes of benefits. Here's a few:

1. **Sleep is improved by grounding:** Grounding aids in the normalization of stress hormones, which helps you sleep better at night. It can even help to alleviate heat flashes. Individuals with sleep difficulties slept under a cotton cover with conductive carbon strands weaved into it in a research published in the *Journal of Alternative and Complementary Medicine*. This was attached to a wire that ran outside to a metal bar buried in the ground. When subjects were grounded,

they slept better and reported less discomfort and tension.

2. **Grounding helps to alleviate pain:** When you ground, moving electrons from the ground make contact with your skin and penetrate your body, functioning as natural antioxidants, according to a study published in the *Journal of Inflammation Research*. They prevent oxidative stress in cells, tissues, and organs. According to a study published in the *Journal of Alternative and Complementary Medicine*, people with muscle discomfort who slept on a grounding device had less inflammation. Grounding also aided faster healing, according to their blood indicators.

3. **Grounding elevates one's mood:** According to researchers, those who frequently practice grounding are more focused, balanced, tranquil, strong, and cheerful. In fact, a study published in *Explore* found that people who had grounding therapy had a better mood, as well as less despair and stress.

4. Grounding is good for your heart: According to a study published in the *Journal of Alternative and Complementary Medicine*, grounding improves heart rate volatility. Participants had bloodwork done after

wearing grounding pads on the palms of their hands and soles of their feet. They had very little red blood cell coagulation after being grounded, according to the findings.

5. **It helps to reduce inflammation:** We now know that severe or chronic inflammation is associated to 90% of all chronic health disorders. One of the quickest methods to deal with this is to ground yourself.

6. **Help with managing stress and anxiety:** As an empath, you will be absorbing a ton of negative energy which may end up causing mental health issues such as anxiety, depression, panic, and more. To combat this, all you need to do is make grounding a part of your daily routine. This will greatly benefit your mental health.

CHAPTER 21
GROUNDING TECHNIQUES

NOW THAT WE'VE tackled the "what" and the "why," let's find out "how." So, what are some grounding techniques that will help you Psychics and Empaths out there? Let's take a look!

Normally, grounding techniques are divided into two major groups. The first being "physical" grounding and the second being "cognitive grounding." These groups then have a list of activities that need to be performed to achieve the desired results.

Physical Grounding

When attempting to re-ground yourself, the first step is to return to your physical body. When choosing a technique, start with the body and work your way up to the brain, which means you should choose instruments that call the body first.

- **Breathe:** Try "Boxed Breathing," which involves breathing in for 4 seconds, holding for 4 seconds, breathing out for 4 seconds, holding for 4 seconds, and so on until you feel as though you've become grounded. You can also contract and release your muscles while breathing, concentrating on the breath and remaining conscious throughout.
- **Stretch**: Light stretches can be done while focusing on your breath and paying attention to the physical feelings that occur from the activity.
- **Exercise:** It is a great method to get back into your body, with an emphasis on the physicality of your efforts. Whether it's simple jumping jacks or a long run on your favorite trail, the sensations of movement on your body can help you recover from a panic attack.
- **Mindfulness:** It's crucial to bring your attention to the current moment, whether through a "5, 4, 3, 2, 1" exercise—where you identify 5 items, 4 different sounds, 3 textures, 2 smells, and 1 taste—or simply by focusing your awareness on the present moment and bodily feeling.

- **Senses:** Concentrate on a specific feeling, such as holding an ice cube and noting how it feels or smelling an essential oil.

Cognitive Grounding

You can consciously distract yourself into reverting to the present if something gets too much for your brain. It's critical to use caution while utilizing distraction as a grounding approach. Distracting yourself too much can be a way of avoiding the problem, so if you use distraction as a grounding approach, make sure you return to it and confront it eventually. You're saving it for later while you're distracted.

Distract yourself by:

- Listening to music, watching TV, or painting
- Having a conversation with a friend or loved one
- Playing with or engaging with a pet

PART SEVEN
WORLD—CRYSTALS

CHAPTER 22
CRYSTAL BASICS

IT'S reasonable to say that stones and crystals have piqued our interest for as long as we've existed as a species. Talismans and amulets have been utilized from the beginning of time, but no one knows how the first of these things were interpreted or used. Natural materials were used to make many of the early products. Mammoth ivory beads, as well as modern beads made from shell and fossil shark's teeth, were discovered in a 60,000-year-old burial in Sungir, Russia.

Crystals were frequently utilized (and are still used) in Traditional Chinese Medicine, which dates back at least 5,000 years. Ancient Egyptian jewelry included lapis lazuli, turquoise, carnelian, emerald, and pure quartz. Some stones were used for defense and cleanliness, while others, such as galena and malachite, were ground to a powder to be used as cosmetics, for example, powder for eyeshadow. As was discovered later in ancient Mexico, green stones were used to represent the deceased's heart and were buried with them.

Many of the names we use now have Greek origins. The ancient Greeks credited crystals with a range of qualities. The term "crystal" derives from the Greek word for stone, which was considered to be water that had frozen so thoroughly that it would still remain solid. Amethyst means "not intoxicated," and it was previously worn as an amulet to ward off intoxication and hangovers. Hematite gets its name from the word "blood," which refers to the crimson coloring it produces when it oxidizes. The ancient Greeks associated iron ore hematite with Aries, the god of war. According to legend, Greek soldiers rubbed hematite on their bodies before battle to make themselves invulnerable.

In 1609, Anselmus de Boot, court physician to Rudolf II of Germany, argued that the virtue of a gemstone is due to the existence of good or malevolent angels. The good angels would grant the jewels a special grace, while the bad angels would lead people to believe in the stone's own endowments rather than God's. He goes on to detail the benefits of certain stones while dismissing the attributes of others as mere superstition.

In the early 19th century, a number of remarkable investigations were conducted to explain the effects of stones on people who claimed to be clairvoyant. The patient appeared to experience not just bodily and emotional changes, but also odors and tastes when different stones were touched.

Gemstones have preserved their value despite the fact that they are no longer used for medical purposes. Jet was often worn by mourners until recently, and garnet was commonly worn during conflict. For her wedding, every female descendent of a local family in southwest England wore an antique moonstone necklace passed down through the generations. This was only recently discovered by one of the family members to be a fertility sign.

Until recently, if not all the way up to the current day, many indigenous societies used gemstones for healing. The Zuni tribe of New Mexico creates stone fetishes that symbolize animal spirits. They were ceremonially "fed" powdered turquoise and pulverized corn. Despite the fact that the mystical practice that surrounds them is no longer extensively practiced, stunning ornate fetishes are nevertheless created to sell and are extremely desirable objects or sculptures. Native American tribes still regard precious stones, particularly turquoise, as sacred. Both Aboriginals and Maoris have stone-related healing and spiritual practices, some of which they share with the rest of the world and others that they keep private.

CHAPTER 23
CRYSTALS AND HEALING

CRYSTAL HEALING IS a type of complementary medicine that uses the use of crystals and other stones to treat and prevent disease. Proponents of this practice claim that crystals act as healing conduits, allowing positive, healing energy to enter the body while bad, disease-causing energy exits.

Crystal and gemstones, according to practitioners of crystal therapy, offer therapeutic abilities. Many websites that promote crystal healing claim that it has a lengthy history, dating back roughly 6,000 years to the ancient Sumerians of Mesopotamia.

For thousands of years, crystals have been treasured for their beauty and healing properties. Semi-precious stones such as lapis lazuli, carnelian, clear quartz, emerald, and turquoise were commonly used in ancient Egyptian jewelry, and sculpted burial amulets from the same gems for protection and well-being. They utilized chrysolite (which is today known as topaz) and peridot to ward off night terrors and evil spirits.

In Switzerland and Belgium, Paleolithic gravesites have been unearthed with jet jewelry. Wearing agate, according to the Bishop of Rennes in the 11th century, would make the wearer acceptable and convincing. Sapphires were used for ecclesiastical rings in the 12th century. In ancient China, emperors were buried in jade armor. In China and South America, it was also used to treat kidney problems.

In 1880, two famous scientists from France, Jacques and Pierre Curie, made a scientific discovery. The Piezoelectric Effect demonstrated what centuries of people had already known since they were impelled to use crystals: crystals expel powers. In a nutshell, piezoelectricity is the electrical charge that forms when pressure is applied to crystals, DNA, and bones. Because of their knowledge of pyroelectricity and crystal structures, they were able to predict behavior in crystals such as quartz, tourmaline, and topaz.

Crystals Used in Ayurvedic Medicine

Ayurvedic medicine (sometimes called "Ayurveda") is one of the world's oldest holistic healing systems. It was invented around 3,000 years ago in India. It's based on the belief that optimal health and happiness necessitate a delicate balance of mind, body, and spirit. Rather than combating disease, its major goal is to promote good health. Treatments, on the other hand, can be customized to address specific health concerns.

Ayurveda emphasizes prevention and encourages people to preserve their health by focusing on life balance, correct thinking, nutrition, lifestyle, and herb use. Ayurveda knowledge enables one to comprehend how to acquire and maintain this balance of body, mind, and consciousness depending on one's own unique constitution, as well as how to make lifestyle changes to do so.

Each person's constitution is made up of a unique pattern of energy—a specific blend of mental, emotional, and physical traits. This constitution is determined at conception by a range of circumstances and remains steady throughout one's life.

Many internal and external influences fight against us to disrupt this balance, resulting in a shift in one's constitution away from the balanced condition. Emotional and physical stresses might include things like mood, diet, and dietary preferences, seasons and weather, physical trauma, and work and family relationships. Once these variables are identified, suitable efforts can be made to reduce or remove their effects, as well as to eliminate the sources of imbalance and return to one's original state.

Crystals have been used in Ayurveda in addition to herbs and other treatments. For thousands of years, Ayurvedic healers and astrologers in India and Tibet have suggested wearing unique gemstones close to the skin for treating ailments, chronic infection, and increasing cosmic vibrations.

In Ayurveda, there are nine primary gems known as "Navaratnas." These nine gems are based on the Navaratnas or Nauratan, a group of nine exceptional persons who lived in an emperor's court in India. Ruby, pearl, coral, emerald, topaz, diamond, sapphire, agate, and cat's eye are the nine gems. In terms of its benefits, each gem has its own value. Here's a list to help you figure out which gemstone is most acceptable for you to wear.

Manakya/Ruby: It has the appearance of a red lotus with a ruby star. The corundum tribe includes ruby, which is an aluminum and oxygen alloy. It is used to treat heart disease, memory loss, and mental diseases such as depression, psychosis, anxiety, and epilepsy, among other things.

Mukta/Pearl: Mukta or Moti, the Moon's stone, is available in a range of shining white lusters. Pearls are biological stones produced by seal oysters. The pearl is prized for its cooling characteristics; thus, it is utilized to soothe the body. The pearl will also aid with eye problems, insomnia, mental weariness, fever, and palpitations.

Praval/Coral: A rich red rose-colored gemstone that resembles ruby in appearance. It's an organic gemstone created from the feces of pravals. It's used to treat heart and brain problems like nausea, asthma, poor blood circulation, and fever.

Panna/Emerald: The therapeutic qualities of this green gemstone are what set it apart. They include the treatment of vomiting, poisoning, liver ailments, fever, piles, and anemia.

Pukhraj/Topaz: This cream-colored stone has therapeutic characteristics that can aid in the treatment of skin conditions, digestive problems, piles, and nosebleeds.

Heera/Diamond: Carbon atoms are organized in a hexagonal crystal lattice to make diamond. It is the most coveted gemstone on the planet. Because the dazzling, gleaming jewel is classified into two categories: male and female, it is advised that you use caution when wearing it. When the polished ash of the beautiful gemstone is used, it can heal a multitude of illnesses by balancing all energy in the body. To acquire essential energy, it can be blended with other ayurvedic rasayans or taken with milk, honey, or butter.

Neelam/Sapphire: The bright blue jewel is a corundum, which is an alloy of aluminum, oxygen, and iron impurities with iron impurities that gives it its color. The stone is considered to cure gastric difficulties, psychological ailments, severe traumas, and eating disorders. In addition, sapphire or neelam is useful for brain problems like mental strain, epilepsy, and depression, as well as delivering happiness and contentment while also boosting brain ability.

Gomed/Agate: This Gomed stone was named because of its resemblance to cow fat. These light-yellow gemstones improve the appearance of the skin and aid in the treatment of skin issues.

Vaidurya/Cat's eye: When light strikes on this gemstone, it creates a centered white streak. Vaidurya (cat's eye) is said to combat the harmful effects of the planet Ketu in Ayurveda. It strengthens the body's defenses by treating disorders of the heart, brain, and body. It also gives you more stamina.

In general, a variety of semi-precious stones are linked to a variety of advantages. Another list of non-Ayurvedic crystals to wear for their various benefits is available here:

Celestite: Its name comes from the Latin word "caelestis," which literally means "heavenly." It makes sense: the stone's celestial blue tint will aid us in achieving the same sensation of calm and happiness that we get from gazing up at the sky on a beautiful day. It's a great crystal to keep in your bedroom to help you get a good night's sleep by bringing peace and harmony to your energy field.

Smoky Quartz: It's an excellent healing crystal for protection since it can act as a shield against negative energies. You will recognize and release stale, sticky behaviors and values that are holding you back while meditating with this gem in your palm. Clearing room for new and more creative energy to come in might be advantageous in terms of energy.

Turquoise: Turquoise, also known as the Master Healer, is supposed to operate as a spiritual link between heaven and earth. Since ancient times, the magnificent blue stone has been revered for its protective and auspicious characteristics. Turquoise is an interaction stone, so it may be able to help you communicate if you're having difficulties putting your thoughts or feelings into words. Turquoise's healing abilities are thought to be increased when given as a present, so give one to a friend or family member who could use some good fortune.

Carnelian: It's a fantastic stone for artists. It can be utilized to dismantle the boundaries that make us feel drained, uninspired, and confined. By simply glancing at it, its vibrant orange color stimulates passion, inspiration, faith, and joy.

Rose quartz: It is a stone of healing and unconditional love. It's claimed to open up the heart chakra and induce forgiveness in both others and ourselves. Check out what occurs when you use this chakra stone to nurture and support yourself on your journey to self-love.

Aventurine: Aventurine, like rose quartz, is said to unlock the heart's energy and can help you overcome emotions of self-doubt and gain confidence.

Clear quartz: One of the most well-known crystals is the transparent quartz crystal. It has long been used to balance the body and calm the mind by ancient societies, and its clear color makes it effective in a variety of situations.

Citrine: It is the crystal of light, happiness, and existence. Holding one serves as a subtle reminder to stay in the present moment and appreciate the world as it is. Citrine is a lovely manifestation stone that encourages us to dream bigger, keep cheerful, and be appreciative in our daily lives.

Bloodstone: It's a powerful energizer, and having one in your hands can help you stay focused while you work toward your goals. If you've reached a personal or professional roadblock and need to get back on track, this is the stone for you. To increase your motivation and morale, place it on your desk or on your altar at home.

Selenite: Selenite crystals, which are commonly used for protection, are supposed to absorb negative energy. Place one on your windowsill to keep negative energy away from your home. Keep it out during the full moon, since this powerful celestial force is thought to cleanse and charge all crystals.

Shungite: It's a calming stone. This weighty, dark, occasionally black stone is useful to keep while meditating to relax your thoughts and anchor oneself.

Black tourmaline: It serves as an energy guardian, and its deep black color can assist deflect negative energy before it enters your life. It's a nice stone to have on hand at home to keep a light and optimistic feeling going.

Amethyst: It's a mythical stone that's said to help people connect to their intuition and open their third eye. It's also linked to mental clarity and psychic powers. Find a quiet place where you can sit for a long amount of time with the stone in your hands to see if any new ideas emerge.

Moonstone: It may be found all over the world and is recognized for its light blue, transparent tints. This stone is thought to be connected to feminine lunar energy, and it's a nice one to keep by your bedside as a reminder to relax and connect with your more intuitive and responsive side before bed.

Anecdotal Evidence of Crystal Healing

It's one thing to read about how crystals can affect you; it's quite another to really feel it. Some of you reading this book may have had similar experiences, heard a few stories, or are simply interested in learning more about them. Here is a collection of stories that may interest you, no matter who you are or what group you belong to.

Let me begin by telling you a story about a young man. He was 18 at the time, and he was juggling college and family obligations. He began missing lectures and examinations, and he was hardly seen at times. That was all until he and his family embarked on this excursion (a weekend in the northern areas of his country). Apparently, he was given the option of picking a stone from a pile. He chose a black tourmaline because of its color and appearance (knowing nothing about it but its name). Later, as he and his family returned to their hotel, he immediately began his investigation and discovered its advantages. He has kept it near to him since that day, believing it was meant to be with him, and has even made it into a necklace that he wears to this day. His life improved; he was happier, more active, resumed his lessons, and was generally more present in the lives of those around him.

The average public has a negative attitude toward crystal therapy. However, it's difficult not to believe that it's all a bunch of nonsense when you see incidents like these.

Let me relate a few more stories similar to the one I described previously to show my argument. A woman was going through a breakup and worried that she had just lost the love of her life.

According to the 34-year-old, she felt as if her world had been smashed into a million pieces. Her shoulders drooped forward under the weight of what she believed was melancholy. Her heart, she believed, had been shattered into a million pieces, and her shoulders had begun to droop forward as a result of the weight she was carrying.

As a result, the girl's companion, who was studying shamanism at the time, placed a string of seven linear energy gateways along her chakras. Some think that crystals' vibrations and therapeutic properties aid in the clearing of leftover negative energy from the chakras and the repair of both body and mind. A friend placed a pale pink piece of rose quartz, also known as the "love stone."

"I recall that weight that was formerly on my heart being removed with a genuine concentrate on the heart chakra, using that rose quartz," the woman said of the event, which she characterized as "life changing."

Madi Skahill, a writer who was dealing with the stress and anxiety of a pandemic-plagued year, looked for a way to help. With the pandemic's isolation and overwhelming, collective loss, as well as the general expectation to be productive and carry on with daily life as if everything is OK, she resorted to crystal healing and sought the advice of a professional in the field. She began the process with skepticism, but toward the end, she said, "I feel like the experience has made me more self-aware, and brought a sense of clarity to the way I'm dealing with challenges in my day-to-day life."

Another woman wrote about her experience of wearing a healing crystal necklace for an extended period of time. She went in with skepticism, believing that the whole thing was a hoax and that "real" treatment was the way to go. She first went to a healer, who recommended crystals that would work best for her. She went on to have more sessions with her healer and began wearing her necklace on a regular basis. At the conclusion of it all, she stated that her perspective about life had changed dramatically, and that she had become more positive, social, and productive in her daily life. She described the situation as "making her feel happy."

If these stories aren't enough to persuade you, celebrities like Bella Hadid and David Beckham could. These celebrities laud the healing properties of crystals, believing that they can bring anything from peace and happiness to reducing tension and even aiding in the treatment of medical issues.

These are only a few occurrences, but there are a plethora of additional stories waiting for you to discover if you are willing to take the plunge. Hopefully, you've been persuaded enough to seek out a crystal healer in your area and get some hands-on experience.

PART EIGHT
AFFIRMATIONS

CHAPTER 24
WHAT ARE AFFIRMATIONS?

AS WE'VE DISCUSSED several times before in this book, empaths, intuitives and psychics are prone to absorbing negative energy. This can have an adverse effect on both their physical and mental health. Gradually they may be faced with low self-esteem. Don't worry though, if you identify as any of the said mystics, we've got you covered! Have you heard of positive affirmations? If you have—amazing! If you haven't, that's okay too. Keep reading on to find out how you can better your mental health with positive affirmations.

An affirmation is a brief yet impactful phrase. They provide you the ability to consciously manage your thinking. Affirmations are carefully crafted in order to have the greatest impact. They become the concepts that mold your world when you express or think about them. They are self-affirming positive phrases that we use to confront problematic thoughts and attitudes.

Many people believe Emile Coue, a French psychologist and chemist, to be the "Father of Affirmations." Coue found in the early 20th century that when he told his patients how successful a potion was as he was giving it to them, the effects were significantly better than if he didn't say anything at all.

He realized that the concepts that fill our minds become reality exclusively, and he invented a sort of autosuggestion in which he asked his patients to repeat to themselves every day, "Every day, in every way, I am getting better and better." Coue's approaches resulted in many spectacular cures throughout the course of his life's work, yet he also failed.

It's easy to practice positive affirmations; all you have to do is choose a sentence and reiterate it to yourself. Positive affirmations can be used to motivate oneself, promote changes that will help, or increase your self-esteem. Positive affirmations can be used to overcome negative self-talk habits and substitute them with more adaptable explanations if you find yourself getting hung up on them constantly.

Positive affirmations could be used as part of the daily routine, such as when you get up or before going to bed, or they can be produced and repeated as needed. Positive affirmations, for instance, can be quite beneficial in providing that extra push if you are feeling down or lacking confidence or concentration. When we recite these affirmations to ourselves repetitively, they get ingrained in our minds, and we eventually believe even more of the wonderful things we tell ourselves. This makes us feel more optimistic and improves our self-esteem.

Affirmations may appear to be unreasonable to you. However, consider positive affirmations in this light: many of us engage in recurrent activities to enhance our overall fitness, and affirmations, similarly, are mental and emotional exercises. Positive mental affirmations can rewire our thinking habits, causing us to think—and act—differently over time.

Research shows that affirmations can assist you do better at work, for example. According to studies, focusing on your finest traits for a few moments prior to a high-pressure event can soothe your anxiety, improve your mood, and raise your odds of a favorable outcome.

Self-affirmation might likewise help to reduce stress's impacts. A quick affirmation exercise improved the problem-solving skills of "chronically stressed" participants to the same degree as those with low stress, according to one experiment. Affirmations have been shown to be effective in the treatment of poor self-esteem, depression, and other psychological issues. They've also been demonstrated to activate the parts of our brains that enable us to make favorable health modifications.

CHAPTER 25
BENEFITS OF POSITIVE AFFIRMATIONS

WHY BOTHER WITH POSITIVE AFFIRMATIONS? Well, here's why!

- You become more conscious of your daily thoughts and words, lowering your chance of allowing negativity to infiltrate your life.
- You begin to see more synchronicities in your life, which encourages and motivates you to continue practicing.
- Daily affirmations not only keep you surrounded by what you desire in life, but they also help you attract additional blessings and presents.
- Keeping the simple things in perspective is easier with daily practice. In today's fast-paced society, it's easy to lose sight of how

big the little things are. When you're healthy, it's easy to lose sight of how fortunate you are. "I am healthy," as a simple morning affirmation sentence, can go a long way.

- According to a new study, those who are optimistic have healthier hearts, and affirmations can help you stay happy.
- Others will notice as you maintain this habit, and you will begin to serve those around you without even trying. As a result, you'll be more concentrated.
- Affirmations on a daily basis maintain you in a constant mood of thankfulness.
- Positive affirmations are especially useful when you're stressed, such as in a social scenario. They'll assist you in overcoming tension and resolving problems.
- If you're using affirmations on a regular basis, you're becoming more self-aware and taking control of your thoughts. This leads to a situation in which you have more mental control and are more conscious of your own wants and needs.

CHAPTER 26
TYPES OF AFFIRMATIONS

ROUTINE AFFIRMATIONS

These are affirmations that you should say on a daily basis. They're fairly generic and sound a lot like goal affirmations. To start the day and get into a specific mindset, you can utilize daily affirmations. Like attaining a goal or changing your mindset. Here are a few examples:

- I am deserving.
- I enjoy being myself.
- Extraordinary things are about to happen.
- I am pleased with myself.
- I'm capable of overcoming any obstacle.
- I am a robust and healthy individual.

Motivational Affirmations

These reminders urge you to work harder by igniting powerful and motivated thoughts. We all need a little push now and then, and that's what these affirmations are for.

- I don't get worked up over minor details.
- I choose happiness today because I am in control of how I feel.
- On the internet, I will not compare myself to others.
- My existence is my strength.
- In everything I do, I am successful.
- What I can accomplish has no bounds.

Affirmations of Self-Love

Affirmations are an excellent technique to increase your self-esteem and love for yourself.

- I'll always look out for myself.
- Every day, I grow to appreciate myself more.
- I've decided to stop being apologetic for who I am.
- I am deserving of good fortune.
- I adore and respect myself for who I am.

Your Finest Characteristics

Recognizing your best traits and working on enhancing others is what confidence is all about. Maybe music is your strong suit.

- I'm a wonderful musician who is improving every day.
- Because my music is amazing, I am deserving of every praise I receive.
- I'm becoming an incredible [something else], much like I'm a good musician.

Visualization Affirmations

The significance of visualization affirmations varies. For example, where do you want to be in a month, a year, or 5 years? Or how will your life be after a particular incident or accomplishment? Here are a few samples that you can tweak to fit your needs.

- My business will grow in popularity and become successful.
- I want to be satisfied with my level of fitness next year.
- My grades will improve by next month because I will study, pay attention, and work more.
- I m going to attempt to be gentler with myself after my birthday.

- I'll attract new possibilities.

Personal Objectives Affirmations

These are comparable to visualizations, except they are more specific. As previously, personalize these affirmations to suit your needs.

- I am going to learn [something] by [a specific time].
- I am capable of achieving anything I set my mind to.
- I have the determination to succeed in.
- I have the ability to effect change.

Gratitude Affirmations

When there's a lot to worry about and so many possibilities to compare yourself to others and focus on what you don't have, remember that you have a lot to be grateful for. On difficult days, it helps you to remember the things you take for granted since they're normal to you but not to others. There is often something for which to be thankful for.

- I am grateful for my job.
- I am grateful for the food I eat.
- I am grateful for the loving people in my life.

- I am thankful for the clothes I have.
- I am thankful for my health.

Your Ideas and Beliefs

Amazing things will transpire if you believe in yourself. The cosmos is brimming with resources just waiting for you to claim them and use them to help you develop and thrive. This type of affirmation helps you reiterate these ideas.

- I was created to be happy. My life's purpose and compass is happiness.
- There are so many people that love and support me. They're my parents, relatives, friends, coworkers, clients, partners, and social ties.
- I am always surrounded by more opportunities than I need.
- I feel I can be whoever or whatever I desire.
- It is a blessing to be able to do what I love and follow my passion and delight.

Validation of Decision-Making

Making a decision helps us feel strong and in control of our lives. Decisions also drive us to take action in order to achieve our goals.

- Every day, I choose to make new relationships and chances.
- Every day, I resolve to go a step closer to my goal.
- I choose to accept every challenge that comes my way as I strive to become the person I was created to be.
- I choose to trust in and follow the spiritual direction that exists inside me at all times.
- Every day of my life, I resolve to follow my passion and bliss and to live in love and joy.

CHAPTER 27
A FEW HOURS OF AFFIRMATIONS

NOW THAT WE'VE established what affirmations are and why they're helpful, here's a little treat for you. Below are different types of affirmations meant for different times, and different goals. These will help you empaths, intuitives, and psychics improve your self-esteem and enrich your daily life.

30 Sleep Affirmations

Before going to bed, say these 30 sleep affirmations.

1. My body and brain are both ready for a break. I'm in my safe haven. Everything will turn out okay.
2. I am thankful for my body, which is now at ease. I'm excited about tomorrow.

3. Today, I gave it my all. I'm all set to be re-energized. Tomorrow is a fresh start.

4. Only joy and optimism exist in my dreams. I have faith in myself.

5. For me, sleeping is a natural state. I'll get a good night's sleep and awake refreshed in both mind and body.

6. My dreams will be filled with peaceful sentiments and hope. I'm in a secure environment where I can sleep.

7. I'm going to let go of all my worries. My eyes are fatigued, and my body and I both need a restful night's sleep.

8. I'm grateful for today, thankful for this bed, and I'm excited for tomorrow.

9. Stress and anxiety have no power over me. I'm going to let go and be at ease. I'm due for a restful night's sleep.

10. This body is one that I adore and embrace. In my dreams tonight, I'll nurse it with loving thoughts.

11. I am grateful for the prospects that have presented themselves to me today. Now I'm going to sleep. My objectives are always reachable in the future.

12. With each and every breath I take, I feel more at ease. I am deserving of pleasant dreams.

I'll get the stuff I've been dreaming about tomorrow.

13. Today has been a long day for me. I'm at ease with everything. After a full night's rest, miracles happen.

14. Over tension and concern, I prefer sleep, rest, quiet, and relaxation.

15. My focus is on mindfulness.

16. For now, I am pleased with myself. The next day will be much better. I am a lovely person. I'm due for a nap.

17. I am deserving of rest, relaxation, and dreaming. My nice wishes will be realized.

18. I've made the decision to stop fretting, stressing, and obsessing on the negative. I'm in a natural state of well-being. My body is deserving of a restful night's sleep.

19. I am in good health, and I will reward my body with a restful night's sleep.

20. My thoughts are overflowing. Tonight, I'm releasing. My brain and body will both shine brightly again tomorrow.

21. In my slumber, I feel secure. My sleep relaxes and energizes me for a brighter day ahead.

22. I'm proud of myself. My mind, soul, and body are all magnificent. I'm going to attract amorous dreams.

23. Sleep helps me to heal.
24. I'm looking forward to a nice, soothing, and peaceful night. With these breaths, I release all tension and stress from my mind and body.
25. Today is over, and I'm going to sleep peacefully. My thoughts are in tune with the inherent state of the cosmos.
26. My eyes are simply closing. I'm looking forward to a restful night's sleep.
27. My restful night's sleep has the potential to dispel my fears, anxieties, and doubts. I'm going to sleep soundly now. In my fantasies, I have faith.
28. My faults today do not define me. I've earned a decent night's sleep. I am deserving of the day after tomorrow.
29. I am deserving of love, tranquility, and sleep.
30. I'm learning, growing, and looking forward to the future. I have faith in myself.

50 Affirmations for Meditation to Feel Positive Energy

This set of affirmations can be practiced during the morning or before an important event to ignite some positivity within your life.

EMPATH & PSYCHIC ABILITIES: 255

1. I am at ease.
2. I am at peace.
3. I am in the "here and now."
4. I am content.
5. My mindfulness is improving with each day.
6. I am capable of making time for me and my necessities.
7. I'm able to take long, steady breaths.
8. Everything in my head is fine.
9. Everything in my life is going smoothly.
10. I'm confident that I'll be able to achieve perfect tranquility.
11. My emotions, thoughts, and actions are all under my control.
12. I am at peace with myself.
13. When I focus, I am at peace.
14. I am dedicated to and concentrating on my mindfulness training.
15. I am robust and tough.
16. I'm being led in the right direction.
17. My natural condition is one of peace.
18. Nothing can disrupt my tranquility.
19. I let go of my stress and worry.
20. My breathing is shallow and slow.
21. My mind and body are both at ease.
22. I'm completely devoted to mindfulness.

23. I am capable of accepting and dealing with anything.
24. My soul and emotions are at ease.
25. I'm exactly where I'm supposed to be at this moment.
26. With each exhale, I let go of tension and stress.
27. I can sense how I'm disconnecting from the outside world and immersing myself in my own thoughts.
28. I'm at ease in my own skin.
29. I am aware of the advantages of meditation.
30. I am aware of the positive energy that exists within and around me.
31. I take a deep breath and inhale peace and harmony. I exhale my concerns and tension.
32. My body is capable of self-healing.
33. My mind and body are intrinsically tied.
34. Every day is a fresh start.
35. Positive energy is all around me.
36. I have a powerful mind as well as a powerful physique.
37. I am filled with wonderful energy.
38. I'm at ease and at peace.
39. Everything is in fine order.
40. I am a source of peace and harmony.
41. I just think about the good things in my life.

42. With each breath, my mind and body heal.
43. In irritating and stressful situations, I can maintain my composure.
44. Every minute of serenity makes me glad.
45. I let go of any thoughts I had prior to meditating.
46. My mind is decluttered.
47. It comes easy to me to become tranquil.
48. All of my problems have passed me by.
49. Nothing can disrupt my tranquility.
50. All areas of my life are under my control.

30 Affirmations to Calm Anxiety and Relieve Stress

If you're feeling particularly stressed out due to any reason, try saying these 30 statements to yourself.

1. I am okay.
2. I have things under control.
3. I am capable of dealing with trouble.
4. Just like in the past, I can get through this.
5. I can get through anything.
6. I am strong.
7. I am smart.
8. I am capable of great strides.
9. No matter the consequences, my efforts will be fruitful.
10. I will leave things to the divine.

11. The divine has my back at all times.
12. The world has a plan for me, one that I may not be aware of at the moment.
13. I will do what I can, then I will wait for the result.
14. Things will turn out the way they're supposed to be.
15. I am at peace with my efforts.
16. I will get things done with my brilliance.
17. My stresses are like water, they will flow away into a stream.
18. I am light, I am free.
19. I am like a bird in the sky soaring high.
20. I am like the sun that comes up every day and lights up the world.
21. I am the moon, who's glow magic happens under.
22. I am a forest, deep and full of life.
23. I am a force of nature, capable of doing anything I put my mind to.
24. I stand tall, just like an ancient oak tree.
25. My roots are resilient, they will carry me through any storm that may come.
26. I am where I need to be.
27. I am capable.
28. I will get through the dark without harm.
29. I have done what I needed to.

50 Affirmations to Aid the Grieving Process.

If you've suffered loss in some way—be it losing a loved one, experiencing heartache, having to say goodbye to a pet, or contracting a chronic illness, these affirmations may come in hand to help with your grief.

1. I have the ability to hang on to love while letting go of grief.
2. I let go of the idea that I've lost everything.
3. I give myself permission to grieve before moving on.
4. As I grieve, I am finding strength in myself.
5. I let go of the notion that this is all too much for me.
6. In any scenario, I can find joy.
7. Slowly, I allow my spirit to heal.
8. I completely adore myself.
9. I'm always on the mend, and I'm never alone.
10. One moment, one step at a time, I'll focus on accepting myself while grieving.
11. I'm still aware of the love that the earth gives.
12. I'll take the positive aspects of this time and move on.

13. All of my sentiments of loneliness and isolation are released.
14. Today, although I weep, I sense the presence of my angels.
15. My heart is content.
16. The cosmos lifts me up, supports me, and lead me in the right direction.
17. I'm guarded and nurtured.
18. There is no one-size-fits-all approach to grieving.
19. Everything is playing out exactly as it should.
20. The blessings of life fill me with eternal appreciation and admiration.
21. When help is offered, I am willing to accept it.
22. I may show my gratitude by living a meaningful life.
23. These life lessons are highly valuable.
24. I've been fractured but not ruined.
25. When I'm in agony, I'll always embrace the support that others have to offer.
26. I free myself of all blame.
27. Every parting is merely the start of something new.
28. I let go of all the stress and anguish that comes with gripping too hard.

EMPATH & PSYCHIC ABILITIES: 261

29. Rather than mourning the loss, I will constantly focus on the potential that each scenario presents.
30. I am ready to let go of any negative, frightening thought from my mind, body, and life.
31. I believe that letting go is a necessary part of life.
32. My pains and sufferings are no longer with me.
33. I've lived and I've loved. Today, I give and receive love.
34. I'll find individuals who will listen and accompany me on this journey through loss.
35. I have the right to take pauses from my pain. Grief drains me completely, and I need to rest in order to move on.
36. I'm becoming better and happier every day.
37. I know I'm strong enough to let go of the anguish I'm holding in my mind, body, and energy field.
38. I let go of all my panicked feelings.
39. I make a list of all the ways I can't seem to get rid of these thoughts.
40. I am the source of my pleasure.
41. I'm not enraged. I'm in a state of mourning.

42. I let go of the idea that I'll never be able to recuperate.
43. I make a list of all the reasons why this shouldn't have happened to me.
44. I make a list of all the ways I'm sinking and fight them off.
45. I am free of the agony of having been deceived.
46. Instead of being distressing, happy memories are becoming comfortable.
47. I'm working on healing my inner kid and reassuring her that she is not alone.
48. I accept what I can't change and summon the confidence to alter what I can.
49. The worse things get, the stronger I become.
50. Sometimes, I may feel empty. Which is okay. My heart is trying to control the uncontrollable.

30 Affirmations That Will Help Empaths.

Bet you didn't expect this, huh? This is a little gift for you. These affirmations are specially written to help all the overburdened empaths out there.

1. I am secure and well-protected by the heavenly.

2. It's none of my concern what they're feeling. I'm aware that I can sense it, yet it's not my responsibility.
3. Rather than analyzing, my gut tells me to trust.
4. I know I can sense this person's anguish, yet there is a moral for them to learn.
5. Just the emotional input that I need to understand and act on is heard, seen, felt, and sensed by me.
6. I only accept energy that is beneficial to me, and I am shielded from all other energies.
7. To treat my dependencies and maintain physical, emotional, and spiritual balance, I will learn self-care.
8. At most occasions, I boost my frequency to assist and nurture myself.
9. I'm trying to let go of the negative energy and sentiments in my life.
10. I give myself permission to let go of bad feelings that no longer benefit me.
11. My sensitivity will be put to good use in my own life and in the world.
12. I sense but do not consume other people's energies.
13. I'll be robbing them of vital knowledge if I jump in.

14. I'm experiencing the fundamental emotions of compassion, serenity, and joy.
15. In my life, I draw only loving and compassionate teachings and connections.
16. I am a shining symbol of hope, peace, and joy.
17. In every scenario, I have the freedom to decide how I feel.
18. As I convey the richness and artistry of my heart, I am exceedingly fortunate and pleased.
19. I'm letting go of the negative energy that has built up in my thoughts.
20. I'll respect others' privacy as much as I respect mine.
21. As I discover what it entails being an empath and accept my skills, I resolve to appreciate my sensibilities and approach myself with kindness.
22. I'm going to allow myself to relax and schedule enough alone time to recover.
23. Anything that isn't mine has been removed from my possession.
24. I'm going to embrace my sensitivity and give myself permission to relax and rejuvenate.

EMPATH & PSYCHIC ABILITIES: 265

25. I express myself honestly and take the time to enjoy my own energy, understand my actual self, and spiritually improve.

26. With my loved ones, I shall convey my emphatic needs. It's cruel to ignore my own feelings.

27. I have to keep in mind that although I can hear their thoughts and feelings, they can't hear mine.

28. When I'm feeling overwhelmed, I'll breathe deeply and exhale to let go of stress and negative energy.

29. I'll work to strike a balance between my intuition and other elements of my life so that I can fully express my range of emotions and be complete.

30. In terms of the connections that are nourishing me, I will trust my gut.

.

PART NINE
SELF CARE FOR MYSTICS

CHAPTER 28
WHAT IS SELF-CARE?

WE DO SO much and ask for little in return. This section is an homage to self-care and techniques to help you treat yourself better.

Many of us learn the value of independence, hard work, and exceeding expectations from a young age. We drive ourselves to achieve greater heights, to accomplish more, and to outperform our colleagues. Few people, however, achieve a life they appreciate by always pushing. As empaths or psychics, we may well be pushing ourselves even more so than our peers.

Self-care is described as the practice of caring for oneself through practices that enhance health and proactive handling of sickness when it strikes. People practice self-care on a daily basis through eating habits, exercise, and sleep. While the notion of self-care has gained popularity over the years, it has a long history. Socrates is attributed with starting the self-care revolution in early Greece, and it is demonstrated that caring for oneself and loved ones came to exist when humankind first came on the planet. Self-care is still the most common type of healthcare around the globe.

Self-care is cultivating a mindset that prioritizes your physical and mental well-being. It manifests itself in a variety of ways, including getting adequate sleep and eating well, and also in several other facets of life, It entails saying "no" to more responsibilities without feeling guilty It's the important of liking yourself and the way you do things, setting limits with family members or acquaintances that consume too much energy, taking a stand for oneself, giving oneself the gift of mindfulness, keeping a nutritious diet, frequently exercising, and prioritizing sleep, requesting assistance without reluctance or embarrassment, and as you strive for your aspirations, treating yourself with care and compassion.

CHAPTER 29
TYPES OF SELF-CARE AND HOW YOU CAN PRACTICE THEM

EMOTIONAL SELF-CARE

These are activities that allow you to connect, process, and reflect on a complete spectrum of feelings.

What can I do?

Engage in an activity that brings you joy.

This could include something as small as going on a walk or as indulgent as taking a fancy vacation to the Bahamas!

Work on your breathing skills.

Breath-work is so important. We've outlined some ways to achieve that in our meditation section. Refer back to that and become a breathing expert.

Only post positive content on social media.

Try not to indulge in content that will make you second-guess yourself and also avoid posting things that may do the same to others. This could mean avoiding overly altering your pictures or lying to get views and likes.

Use adult coloring books to relieve stress and anxiety.

Some that can be especially beneficial for empaths are those that feature mandalas. As per Carl Jung, mandalas are an excellent way to express your emotions.

Practice mindfulness techniques.

Again, go over to our meditations section where you can find mindfulness meditation described in length.

Say positive affirmations over and over.

We've got you covered here as well. Go through our list of positive affirmations and begin your day with a healthy mindset.

On a weekly basis, set new goals.

These can take the form of cutely designed to-do lists or even notes in your smartphone.

Write.

Be it journaling, fictional writing, poetry, or lists—any type of writing will help you put your emotions into words.

Make a collage with encouraging images.

Use Pinterest or a physical board. It is famously said that "A picture is worth a thousand words." As an empath, flooded with emotions and energies, you may have a hard time articulating your feelings, images and visuals could be very helpful in this scenario.

Give yourself permission to communicate all of your feelings in a safe setting.

This could be done with a trusted friend or family member. This could also be with a therapist or any mental health professional.

PRACTICAL SELF-CARE

These are tasks you finalize that satisfy fundamental areas of life in an attempt to avoid potential stressful circumstances.

What can I do?

Save money.

This is an important part of practical self-care. Do not overspend, be it crystals or tarot cards, try to spend less and save money that you could use in an emergency. This would alleviate some financial stress.

Invest in life and health insurance.

A lot of people avoid investing in insurances, but in truth, these can be valuable forms of self-care. You are essentially creating a safety net for your being. This could help you relieve stress in the future.

Spend time and money on education.

Knowledge is the most valuable asset one can purchase. Knowledge is power and it is the highest form of self-care. In this book, we do not think that ignorance is bliss. The more you learn, the better you can live your life. So, go on and spend on your education.

Organize your surroundings.

This cannot be stressed enough. Organizing your home space and work space is more important than it may seem. It can help you navigate through your things easily and get more work done. Organized spaces equal to an organized mind.

Live in a home that's for you, and not a show-off.

Often people spend tons of money on living spaces that are extravagant and aesthetically pleasing; however, they lack a sense of homeliness. Build a home that is your safe haven, a comfortable space for you to unload and not a mansion that would make you feel lonelier and leave you with an empty bank account.

Use technology, but not too much.

Using technology is an essential part of daily life. Whether it is you taking online classes via zoom, or talking to family that's abroad. However, it is essential to limit how much you indulge in technology. It not only costs a lot of money but can be damaging to your mental and physical health.

Be consistent with your responsibilities.

Whether it is work, or social relationships, the better you are at managing your responsibilities, the better the outcome will be. For example, if you care for your siblings in the intended way, they will care for you when you are in need. Similarly, if you handle your work with the utmost care, you are likely to receive monetary gains.

Record memories in some way.

This could be through taking photographs, or writing accounts of moments that brought you joy.

These memories can then be passed onto the following generations making your legacy live on.

They could be a source of joy and hope for people who see or read them.

Don't rush into things.

Take your time to make decisions, your life is infinitely valuable and therefore it is up to you think things through so as to avoid getting into harm's way.

Be present.

Take this as you will. Whether being present is noticing your surroundings, living in the moment, or paying attention to details. Being present will only help you.

PHYSICAL SELF-CARE

These can be activities that will enhance your physical health and overall well-being.

What can I do?

Eat nutritious meals.

Having a healthy diet is something that cannot be stressed enough. It will improve your health, body image, mood, and overall view of the world. This, however, does not mean to go on diets, only drink green smoothies, or starve yourself. It means being on a balanced diet that will fulfil all your nutritional needs.

Participate in physical activity.

People often mistake exercise with strenuous workouts that last hours and make you not want to leave the bed for several days following it. That is not the case. Exercise can be simply walking or jogging or even skipping rope. If you want, you can definitely hit the gym but the main goal is to not leave your body idle for too long.

Take a stroll.

Long walks have often been depicted as a time of profound thoughts and ideas, and surely, they can be. Try going on walks near forests where there is plenty of oxygen to go around. This will expand both your mind and lungs.

Drink plenty of water.

Drink plenty of water. There isn't a need to explain this. A healthy body equals a healthy mind. Our body is made up of 70% water and thus needs an ample supply of water to function properly. Try drinking about 2 to 3 liters of water daily.

Maintain decent sleeping habits.

The pandemic has added chaos to all of our sleeping patterns but it is absolutely essential to sleep at night and stay awake during the day. Try going to bed at around 10 or 11 pm and wake up around 7 to 8 am. Eight to 10 hours of night sleep will be your best friend. If you're having trouble with sleep, refer back to our sleep affirmations in the affirmations section, they will definitely help you improve your sleep cycle.

Make yourself a cup of tea.

Herbal teas are packed with antioxidants which help with your physical health, they can speed up your metabolism and aid in digestion. It is no secret that a healthy gut can help relieve you of several mental disturbances such as anxiety and depression.

Place yourself in the sun.

Besides the fact that being in the sun elevates your mood, it provides you with vitamin D, which is essential for the bones. Good bone health enables you to be more physically active and do whatever your heart desires.

Shower or take baths regularly.

You obviously need showers for hygiene, but sparkly bubble baths can be a wondrous self-care activity. There is not much a glass of wine in a warm bath can't cure.

PSYCHOLOGICAL SELF-CARE

Any exercise that engages your mind or intelligence is categorized as psychological or mental self-care.

Stay away from toxic people.

It's to keep your sense of self alive. If you allow toxic people into your life, you will waste time analyzing your own behavior in comparison to their toxicity. In short, they like nothing more than bringing you down. So, surround yourself with positive people. This will assist you in becoming a good person. Things that happen around you have an impact on your mind and thus keeping yourself in the company of toxic individuals causes depression and anxiety.

Take a nap without feeling guilty.

If you're feeling bad about napping during the day, naps have been proven to improve happiness, productivity, and creativity, as well as your learning and memory skills. In addition, those who napped for at least 45 minutes had lower blood pressure in relation to mental stress than those who did not nap, according to research.

Examine your negative thoughts.

It is critical to attempt to recognize unfavorable thought processes. It's important to review these thoughts from a bird's eye perspective since we can become trapped perceiving negative or stressful situations in the same manner without examining the evidence for that interpretation.

Get in the habit of saying "no."

It's critical to be able to say no so that you may feel liberated while also keeping your friendships. Saying no allows you to set healthy boundaries while also letting people know what they may expect from you. Gaining clarity on the types of things to which you wish to say yes is a beneficial method for making it easier to say no. Make a list of your top priorities and keep it somewhere you'll see it often.

Create a mental health workbook.

Workbooks for mental health can help you process your experiences, learn about your own psychology, and frequently uncover skills and tools to aid you in your daily life. They can add to your mental health toolkit by offering a variety of approaches, scientific research, and a safe place for you to express yourself.

Change it up and break up your routine.

Switching up the routine and including something interesting that you enjoy doing can assist to make your day more enjoyable and entertaining. This happiness can help to boost brain function by allowing one to take a break from the routine and enjoy themselves.

Reshape your brain by listening to binaural tones.

According to certain studies, listening to specific binaural tones can boost the strength of specific brain waves. Different brain processes that control thought and feeling might be increased or inhibited as a result of this.

Pick up a book and read it.

Reading is not only a fun way to stay entertained while socially isolating yourself, but it has also been found to boost general mental health. There is a book for everyone out there, from memoirs to romantic fiction.

SPIRITUAL SELF-CARE

Spiritual self-care activities are those that will nourish your soul and help you to think beyond yourself. Spiritual self-care is not always religious.

Engage in yoga.

Yoga's goal is to bring your body, mind, and spirit into harmony, and it's tailored to your specific needs at the time. The physical benefits of yoga are well-known, but it offers much more than a solid workout. It allows you to connect with your body and deep-seated emotions. Yoga teaches nonjudgment and acceptance of where you are in life while also emphasizing the importance of laying a firm foundation for a more fulfilling existence.

Take a moment to meditate.

Meditation is among the most simple and accessible spiritual traditions. It may take some persuasion to begin, but once you do, it's difficult to fathom life without it. Meditation has various advantages, including stress reduction and a better understanding of what you're doing and also what you need out of life.

Take a mindful walk.

Walking is underappreciated. Walking has been shown to be beneficial to those with mental health issues in studies. Walking, more than any other sort of physical activity, is helpful. It helps you to put life on hold and focus solely on the present moment. Breathing in fresh air, feeling the concrete beneath your feet, and looking up at the vastness of the sky are all subtle methods to ground and nourish the senses. Walking with awareness is a discipline that has a slew of advantages that may surprise you.

Clear space for yourself.

Maintaining clean, open space around you is an excellent practice generally. You're continuously sharing emotions and knowledge with others, so it's only natural that you'll be influenced in certain ways. When you're exhausted or drained, it's difficult to connect with your inner self. Smudging with a specific incense, such as sage, cedar, or palo santo, is an excellent way to cleanse your home. It helps, whether it be the uplifting effect of aroma or the aim of eliminating negative energy.

Participate in the community.

Humans are social creatures by nature. Society may provide you with a sense of belonging, enjoyment, flow of ideas, moral support, and the strength to endure. If you don't yet have these relationships, you may need to take a risk and seek them out. Volunteer, meet others who share your interests, go to religious or cultural events, hold your own meetings, join a book club, or go to a game night. It will be worthwhile to put out the effort.

Keep a journal.

Another approach to dig into the deep corners of your mind and heart is to write. Feelings and emotions are sifted and processed via the process of writing. Problems, fears, and unpleasant emotions can clog your thoughts and make you feel down. Make a list of everything and observe what happens. It's possible that new information will emerge. Journaling can be a great way to add variety to your daily routine. You can experiment with different writing approaches to see what works best for you.

Read motivating content.

This may appear simple, yet it can have a significant impact on your attitude on life. Take note of what you're subjected to on a regular basis and how it affects you. You're bombarded with information from a variety of outlets, and it isn't all good. Consequently, it could be difficult to feel motivated or elevated at times. Make an effort to keep a novel or other form of literature that stimulate you in your bookcase or bedside. Instead of worrying about your day and any anxieties prior to bedtime, make your final ideas pleasant. Trying to read just a few pages first early in the morning might also be a pleasant way to begin the day.

Make an effort to forgive.

Life is far too brief and precious to be locked in routines that aren't serving you. It prevents you from truly appreciating life if you are unwilling to forgive people. Substantial energy is wasted on holding on to resentment or something like that, though that energy may be better spent on building the lifestyle you desire. The sense of freedom and lightness that you will experience can be life-altering.

If you're reading this, you've been on one hell of a journey. You've learnt if you are an empath, or have intuition or psychic abilities. You've discovered what an HSP is and what challenges one may face. You then went on a spiral of learning about different activities that will help you live a healthy life as a mystic.

As you unravel through this journey, remember to know your worth and to indulge in all the activities that this book has led you to.

As a final affirmation to end your journey:

> *Know that you are*
> *Strong*
> *Worthy*
> *Deserving of Love*
> *And on a path of Divination.*

Made in the USA
Las Vegas, NV
25 November 2022